The Intelligence of Feeling

THE INTELLIGENCE
of
FEELING

ROBERT W. WITKIN

HEINEMANN EDUCATIONAL BOOKS
LONDON

Heinemann Educational Books Ltd

LONDON EDINBURGH MELBOURNE AUCKLAND TORONTO
SINGAPORE HONG KONG KUALA LUMPUR
IBADAN NAIROBI JOHANNESBURG
LUSAKA NEW DELHI

ISBN 0 435 80937 7
© Robert W. Witkin 1974
First published 1974

Monotype set in 11 on 12pt. Garamond
Published by Heinemann Educational Books Ltd
48 Charles Street, London W1X 8AH
Printed in Great Britain by Butler and Tanner Ltd
Frome and London

Contents

At sixteen I came across Descartes' dictum 'Cogito, ergo sum'. I took it at once to old Les who used to help us examine such things.

'I think therefore I am,' I announced. There was a pause.

'I feel therefore I am,' he replied quietly.

I knew then that here was a beginning to the matter.

This book is dedicated with the deepest gratitude to Dr. Leslie Ralph, friend and philosopher.

Introduction

This book is concerned in large part with the actions of teachers who teach the creative arts in schools. Above all it is concerned with their consciousness in respect of what they do, the meanings with which they invest their actions in both devising and deploying CURRICULA in the teaching situation.

The elements that go to make up the meaning of action for any individual may be divided *for analytical purposes* into two distinct levels of meaning, the *'theoretical'* and the *'existential'*. The 'theoretical level of meaning' comprises those presuppositions and assumptions, both implicit and explicit, with which the actor constructs the more general and invariant characteristics of both his situation and his functioning within it. Thus underlying a doctor's practice there are a great many presuppositions about the nature of the doctor–patient relationship which enable him to experience aspects of his behaviour as invariant across a wide range of different doctor–patient relationships. In other words these presuppositions hold for all of them. They include the ethical principles of his profession, his general ideas about method and approach to illness, prevention, diagnosis, etc., a great many implicit ideas about life and human relationships, etc., of which he may be only dimly aware, and indeed all of those presuppositions and assumptions that invest his behaviour with consistency and render him recognisable both to himself and others as a doctor.

The 'existential level of meaning' comprises the actor's immediate experience of events in all their particularity consequent upon his functioning in the environment. Thus the thoughts and feelings evoked within the medical man as he actually goes about the business of treating patients, his sensations of adequacy and inadequacy, his immediate experience in the daily business of his life; all go to make up the existential level of meaning for him.

Both levels of meaning are essential to the actor since in order to act he must both experience the reality of his functioning in the environment and at the same time structure that reality in a coherent and consistent way. It is true that we can all act blindly or impulsively at times but we cannot sustain projects in the world on such a basis. Intelligent action is both organised and adapted and it is here that the interrelationship of the two levels of meaning is of such importance. The relationship is in some ways analogous to that between a theory and its empirical testing. The theoretical level of meaning is used as a sort of general 'theory' of action which must be squared continually with the real empirical facts of action in the world. When our empirical experience (the existential level of meaning) can no longer be squared with our ideas of the more invariant aspects of ourselves and our functioning (the theoretical level of meaning) then action begins to lose its coherence for the actor and if nothing is done about it it breaks down altogether. In such a case the theoretical level of meaning for the actor has broken down before the facts and as a consequence it no longer provides an adequate basis for organising action.

When a theory breaks down before the facts in the physical sciences, the scientist has to revise it or abandon it altogether in favour of an alternative. The same is true of ordinary human action in an even more urgent and pressing sense. If our doctor finds that his daily experiences arising from the actual practice of medicine no longer square with his fundamental presuppositions about himself and his funtioning as a doctor, then the latter will cease to enable him to make sense of his daily activity and that same activity will fragment his experience of himself as an integrated human being. In so far as he depends upon his fundamental presuppositions both to guide his encounters in the real world and to make sense of the resulting experience, he must radically revise them when they cease to serve him in this capacity. Failure to do so leads ultimately to action breaking down.

It is necessary to draw some distinction, however, between the term 'theory' as I have used it in respect of the theoretical level of meaning for an actor and the term 'theory' as it is more commonly used in science. In the latter case the term has a more restricted meaning, referring to explicitly formulated hierarchical systems of interrelated propositions from which one can derive empirically testable hypotheses. Theoretical meanings for the actor on the other hand comprise not only knowledge of the propositional type but also general predispositions of a perceptual and sensory/emotional type. That is to say that there are consistencies and generalities in both emotional and perceptual responses that underly the individual's experience of himself and his functioning as well as consistencies of the rational intellectual kind. Thus the apprehensiveness with which one actor approaches a whole range of different interactions is no less an element in his theoretical level of meaning for being a qualitative and feeling disposition. Emotional and perceptual dispositions join rational presuppositions in making up the actor's theoretical level of meaning. They all go together to provide in his experience of himself and his functioning a consistency, an invariance in the face of the variegated contents of his real world. Our presuppositions concerning such things as space, time, human relationships, thinking, feeling, etc., bestow consistency upon our world whether or not we are consciously aware of them. Often we are quite unaware of them. Nevertheless, action in the world is guided by them and they are existentially tested as a consequence. As Nietzsche so rightly pointed out, the question of whether or not some precept is true is answered by, 'Can I live it?' It is in this sense that I refer to the consistencies and general dispositions underlying action as 'theoretical'.

One important way in which the actor's theoretical level of meaning does resemble theoretical constructs in science is that both are essentially conservative. Once established they have a tendency to preserve themselves because they lead the actor to seek out experience for himself which is not disjunctive with his presuppositions. Thus the actor can always confirm the truth of his presuppositions provided they circumscribe his contacts with reality. Of course there are real limits to the power of any set of presuppositions to do this and when the demands of action force the actor to go beyond them in his contacts with reality then the process is begun whereby old theories die and new ones are born.

This book is premised upon the belief that at the present time in the educational world and in society as a whole we are being forced to go beyond our presuppositions concerning our use of expressive media. Teachers of the creative arts (music, fine art, drama, dance, creative writing, etc.) have been experiencing this process for some time. It has resulted in wide and ever speedier swings from one set of theoretical assumptions to another and in a growing feeling of fragmentation and inconsistency as a consequence. In their search for a more adequate basis for action, teachers of the creative arts have become more aware and more critical of existing theoretical meanings.

To comprehend the way in which teachers construct reality in the situation in which they operate, the social scientist must enter into a real dialogue with them in which he can come gradually to frame his enquiry in terms that are relevant to both his own presuppositions and those of the teachers themselves about the same empirical reality, namely the world of the teachers. Such a dialogue must of necessity be mobile and flexible because the social scientist needs continually to restructure his enquiry in process as it were. He must expose his own presuppositions and theoretical notions as part of the very process of sensitising himself to those of the individuals whose consciousness and practice he is studying.

The enquiry which informs this book took the shape of just such a mobile and flexible dialogue with teachers (and pupils) both in and out of schools over a period of three years. In that time I sought to sensitise myself to the consciousness and practice of teachers in respect of the curricula they devise and deploy. My own presuppositions, the conceptual framework within which I was operating, concerned the nature of expressive activity as such and its function in consciousness. My ideas on this emerged from a critical involvement that I have had for some years with the genetic epistemology of Jean Piaget. My primary concern therefore was with the educational function of the creative arts, with the part that they play in the knowledge process and consequently in the developing experience of the child. I entered the field of enquiry with a loosely formulated psychological theory of the relationship between art making and the structuring of the individual's responses. During the course of the dialogue with the arts teaching world I began to clarify my own theoretical ideas as I encountered those of teachers and educators and with that clarification the theoretical presuppositions and dispositions of teachers became clearer to me. Throughout the dialogue, in interviews, conferences, and private discussions, I sought in the very process of questioning to expose my presuppositions as far as possible to teachers and to encourage them both to reveal their own presuppositions and to talk out basic contradictions. In this way I have done my best to ensure that the data collected emerged from dialogue in which, with respect to the matter under discussion, the individuals participating understood one another.

While an attempt was made to quantify some material in connection with questionnaire data, my primary concern in this book has been to provide a depth analysis of the consciousness and practice of teachers of the creative arts in the light of my conceptual framework concerning the function of expressive activity in the developing experience of the child. As the study proceeded, however, and problems of data collection gave way to problems of analysis and exposition it became clear to me that no ordinary social science format would suffice.

A primary objective of the work is that of providing a more thoroughgoing conceptual framework with which to comprehend the use of expressive media and their adaptive function, one that might conceivably provide a more effective basis for action in the teaching of the different creative arts. Such a framework, if it is to be effective, must make sense of the teacher's real experience as it is now and help to resolve contradictions that emerge in that experience with which his own presuppositions are unable to cope. It must enable him to become aware of his own presuppositions in the very process of transforming them. The book itself, however, is essentially a work in social and psychological science. The conceptual framework referred to is an explicit formulation of a psychological theory of expressive action and the analysis of teaching embodies a sociological (and social psychological) mode of enquiry. Potentially, therefore, the book is relevant to an unusually wide range of readers. At one end of the spectrum is the social scientist and at the other the practising teacher. It is hardly surprising, therefore, that the book is quite unlike the type of work that either a social scientist or a practising teacher is accustomed to read.

The reader will find the book more rewarding if he approaches it without pigeon-holing it in advance or seeking to identify it closely with other works that he may have read. I would even suggest that it is best read with a certain innocence in the first instance. Innocence is in no way synonymous with naïveté. There is no suspension of critical appraisal but in the innocent attitude criticism is fresh, genuinely felt and immediate; it is not formalised and dogma-bound. The former type of critical appraisal both leads to and emerges from a genuine engagement with the material. This is all the more true in respect of the present work because I have sought to maintain in the exposition something of the intimate identification in consciousness between social scientist and teacher that characterised the collection of the data. To permit this, I have deliberately excluded scholastic elaboration and almost all academic references.

The book takes the reader from an intensive conceptual analysis of expressive activity through the actual practice of arts teachers to a consideration of possibilities for curriculum development in the creative arts. The layout of the book is quite simple. Part One, THEORY, contains two chapters. The first, entitled 'Knowing, Self, and Being', is designed to engage the reader's fundamental presuppositions, implicit or explicit, about the very nature of 'creative' activity and its origins. Fundamental categories like 'Knowing', 'Self', and 'Being' are derived directly from a consideration of their roots in ordinary human behaviour thereby demystifying the higher mental functions (those used in art making for example) by making them intelligible in terms of the general problems of human adaptation and development. The second chapter of Part One, 'From Beyond the Expressive Act', makes use of the framework in a largely implicit way to explore the logic that underlies the teaching process and the develpment of arts curricula. In the process of exploring the logical foundations of the practice of arts teachers a language is devised for talking about all the different creative arts (music, fine art, dance, drama, creative writing etc.) in terms of common dimensions. The lack of such a language and of a clear conception of educational objectives has contributed greatly to the present weakness of the creative arts in education.

In Part Two, PRAXIS, the results of an empirical research programme into the teaching of English, music, art, and drama/dance in schools are made use of to follow the argument of Part One through the consciousness of teachers and pupils themselves as reflected in intensive interviews and, in the case of the pupils, questionnaire data. Each of four arts selected has a chapter devoted to the teachers studied, and there is one chapter devoted entirely to the pupils' responses.

Part Three, RESOLUTION, is the shortest of the three parts, consisting as it does of only one chapter 'From within the Expressive Act'.

Building upon the work of the first two parts it offers an approach to curriculum development in the creative arts. It presents a conceptualisation of the creative process in terms of three distinct phases and provides suggestions and possibilities for organising curricula and developing methods that comprehend these three phases in ways that permit the teacher's practice to become truly effective in respect of the pupil's expressive act.

I am deeply conscious of the fact that although I have written this book and must take responsibility for its content and style of presentation, it could not have been produced without the investment of quite considerable material and human resources on the part of others. For the material resources and a deal of human patience I have to thank the *Schools Council*. I collected all the empirical material used in Part Two of the book while acting in my capacity as research director of the Schools Council curriculum project 'Arts and the Adolescent'. It was largely thanks to the financial support of the Council that the dialogue with teachers (and therefore the whole enquiry) took place.

On the personal front I could hardly be more indebted to Malcolm Ross, the project organiser. It was he who first introduced me to the arts teaching world and sustained me with his conviction that my ideas had relevance for the problems of arts teachers. Next to Malcolm, I am indebted most profoundly to the hundreds of teachers who lent their consciousness to build this book. The words of some are used here for illustrative purposes in Part Two. Hundreds more who are not quoted nevertheless contributed enormously to the argument.

There are so many people whom I ought to thank but I will confine myself to mentioning those intimate few who lived so closely with the research project—our secretaries and personal assistants Elizabeth Fyffe and Alma Craft who doubled up as 'stabilisers' when the ship hit temperamental turbulence; our research assistants Colin Vyvian and Alison Baker—the brunt of the front line work with the pupils in the schools was borne by them; Joan Entwistle and Gillian Skinner for their dedication to the data processing; my brother Thames for hours, weeks and months of patient transcription, coding, and abstraction. Special thanks are due to Peter Cox, the Director of the project and the Principal of Dartington College of Arts where the project originated. Thanks are due also to Sue Ridler who typed the manuscript. Finally, I must thank my wife

Jackie. She has lived closer than anyone to the struggle for this book, sharing deeply with me the costs of sustained creative enterprise on someone else's time.

R. WITKIN

1 Knowing, Self, and Being

There is a world that exists beyond the individual, a world that exists whether or not he exists. The child needs to know about this world, to move in it and manage himself in it. The curricula of our secondary schools are filled with this world. Everywhere the child turns he encounters it in the brute facts of history, chemistry, mathematics, and so forth. There is another world, however, a world that exists only because the individual exists. It is the world of his own sensations and feelings. He shares the former world with others. He moves around it with them, for it is a world of facts, of public space and 'objects'. He shares the second world with no-one. It is the world of private space and of the solitary subject. In order to move around the world of objects, to manage his relationships within it, the individual must be able to manage the disturbances, the sensations and feelings wrought within him by his encounters in the world. Adaptation implies not only that the individual is able to relate one fact to another or to grasp logical sequences. It implies also that the individual is able to relate personally to the world in which he moves. If his existence in the world disturbs his being in ways that fragment him and render his relationships in the world emotionally confused or even meaningless, then he is ill-adapted, and no amount of intellectual grasp of logical or factual relationships will change that.

If the price of finding oneself in the world is that of losing the world in oneself, then the price is more than anyone can afford. Psychological systems require energy to move them as assuredly as do physical systems. In the case of the psychological system, it is the integrity of the world within the individual that is the source of his motivation, his enthusiasm, his feeling response to life. The more complex and object-ridden man's existence becomes, the greater is the threat to this world within him and the more insistent are the demands of that world as a consequence. The repression of subjectivity in our own age has served only to render its periodic outbursts sharper than ever and to make of subjectivity a topic of special attention and study, as is reflected in books like the present one. This is all the more so because in the severe objectification of our existence the repression has taken a peculiar form. We have not denied the claims of feeling. On the contrary, we have solemnly endorsed these claims. Our problem is that we have forgotten what they are. The task of remembering must begin again in earnest, for the adolescents in our schools are some way on in trying to recover the world of feeling, the subjective life. Often their predicament leads them into forms of behaviour that are regarded by the majority as socially deviant. Whether they are 'beatniks', 'junkies', 'dropouts', 'beautiful people' or just plain dreamers, they have one thing in common. Theirs is the problem of becoming subjective, of becoming persons. It is the problem of Everyman threatened with suffocation by objects that include him as an object. It is the problem of insisting upon oneself.

Our first task must be to establish a way of conceptualising subjectivity, one that does not resort either to mystification or ambiguity. This is important because the creative arts have an especial significance in respect of the world within the individual, in respect of his subjectivity. Only when the significance is grasped as objective fact will the means be at hand for generating new resources for the enrichment of arts curricula and for changing the entire status of the creative arts in schools. Arriving at an adequate conceptualisation of subjectivity, however, requires that we look again at some very fundamental aspects of the child's mode of knowing the world and of knowing his being in the world.

Action as projection through media

All behaviour takes place in an environment, in a medium. I wave my arms about in the air, I displace objects in the room, I swim in the water, I bring about changes in the mind of a listener. My behaviour is registered in the displacements that it causes in the various media, the water, the air, the room or the mind of the listener. The term media is used here to refer to any specific part of the environment in which action takes place and it subsumes not only the physical world but the symbolic world as well. Our environment is made up of symbolic 'objects' as surely as it is made up of physical 'objects' and any account of action must be capable of dealing adequately with both. The elements of a medium that are displaced by my behaviour consist, therefore, of physical objects or symbolic objects.

It would not be possible, however, for behaviour to displace elements in its medium effectively if the behaviour did not itself respond to the specific properties of the objects it displaced. An angular stone resists attempts to roll it along the ground in a way that a perfectly round stone does not. Whether I roll the stone or practise some other method of moving it, depends on the specific properties of the stone. My behaviour in respect of objects becomes 'shaped up' in response to the specific properties of the objects. Another way of putting it is to say that the objects displace elements in the medium of my behaviour.

Here we must introduce a simple distinction between 'behaviour' and 'action'. Behaviour is the raw material of action. It consists of the 'movements' that the individual makes prior to those movements being shaped in the adaptation process. Once behaviour is adapted in its medium it becomes action. In other words, action is here defined as adapted behaviour. I am aware of two objections that may be raised against my definition as a consequence of the ways in which 'action' and 'adaptation' are frequently talked about. In the first place, many people include within their notion of action some element of conscious determination. Human beings act, but other animals behave. The lower we travel down the phylogenetic scale the less are we inclined to speak of an organism's behaviour as action except when we do so in an anthropomorphising sense. Nevertheless, without defending the position fully here, I shall assert my belief that it is more profitable not to use consciousness or intention as a defining characteristic of action. As will be apparent in the ensuing analysis, I take the view that there is no real break between physical and mental acts as such although mental representation as a higher form of action fundamentally transforms the adaptational problem. A second objection to my definition might be that by restricting the term action to 'adapted' behaviour, there is implied some notion of passivity in action in the sense of behaviour being shaped purely at the dictate of environment. It should be apparent as the analysis proceeds that adaptation has quite a different meaning from this and is in no way synonymous with 'conforming' or 'falling into line'. It describes the process of equilibration between a behavioural medium (physical or mental) and an environmental medium (real or symbolic) resulting from the interaction between the two. We may illustrate the process with the following concrete instance.

When a person first attempts to propel himself through water that is too deep for him to stand in, he soon discovers that the water resists all of his normal movements. He cannot walk in it nor can he part it or sweep it to one side. If he is to overcome the resistance and to move through the water then he must organise his behaviour to take account of the specific properties of water. He must learn to swim. Just as the water displaces elements in his behavioural medium producing the action that we call swimming, so his behaviour displaces elements in its environmental medium, namely the water.

Environment and behaviour are two media that interact with one another to produce action. The elements of one displace the elements of the other. We will refer to this process of displacement as 'projection'. The environment is projected through the medium of the individual's behaviour in respect of it and that same behaviour is projected through the medium of the environment. If we return to the illustration of swimming, the behaviour of the individual is projected through the medium of the water, i.e. it displaces the water, and at the same time the specific properties of the water are projected through the medium of the individual's behaviour, i.e. they displace his behaviour thereby shaping up his behaviour to take account of them.

In my terms, therefore, action consists of projections through media. More precisely, it consists of the projection of a behavioural medium by its environmental medium and vice versa. *Both* environment and behaviour are modified in the mutual displacement that produces action.

'Subject response' and 'object response'

The behavioural medium of which we have been speaking comprises the individual's behaviour in respect of objects both physical and symbolic. These objects make up the environmental medium. There are two poles to behaviour and the distinction between them with respect to action is fundamental in the analysis that follows. We usually think of behaviour in its active aspect as something we do in the environment; in our terms as something that displaces elements in the environment as the movement of my hand displaces the air about me or any light object that it encounters. However, my

4

behaviour consists not only of my displacings of 'objects', of the disturbances I bring about in the environment; it consists also of the disturbances that are evoked within me, the disturbances of my being which I experience as sensate impulse. Indeed it is only because my being in the world is disturbed that I am able to act at all. Behaviour as sensate impulse, as disturbance evoked within me, provides the energy for behaviour as active displacement of elements in my environment. Both my sensing and my active displacement of elements in the environment are 'responses', but I shall term the former *'subject response'* and the latter *'object response'*. Subject response consists solely of the disturbing of my being, of my sensing, of the movement of feeling within me which I alone can know. Object response consists of my displacements of objects, even my displacements of myself taken as an object. It should be apparent that there is no behaviour or action in the world that does not partake of both these behavioural aspects in some degree and in some determinate relationship to one another. My existence in the world provokes both sensing within me and action in respect of the world. These are the twin poles of my response. It is my sensing which is the source of all my motivation, of my energy to behave, while it is my behaviour in displacing objects (symbolic or real) that utilises this energy, at the same time bringing me into contact with new objects that evoke new sensing and so forth. Whatever sensations, feelings or emotions that I experience, from the most basic to the most elaborate, they consist of disturbance within me which provides the energy, the motivation to behave in respect of physical or symbolic objects. I act in the world because my being is disturbed in the world.

'Expressive action' and 'impressive action'

If I jump for joy, pull my hat off my head, hurl it in the air and dance on it when it lands on the ground, my actions in respect of the hat are very much under the control of my joyous feeling. Indeed they express that feeling. My joy has full reign. It vents itself uninhibitedly upon my hat and anything else around. People observing me would say that I was acting impulsively, and they would be right. My action is the expression of an impulse, 'joyous impulse'. My behaviour in respect of the hat releases that impulse, it expresses it in a 'feeling-form'—a hat dance no less! Let us suppose, however, that instead of removing my hat in this abandoned manner, I take it off carefully, and positioning it with some accuracy I aim it at a nearby hatstand, release it, and it hits its mark. Obviously there is some impulse there which moves me to propel the hat at the hatstand, otherwise I would not do it, but my behaviour in respect of the hat and the hatstand is very much under the control of their specific properties as objects. The lightness of the hat, the stiffness of the brim and its disc-like shape, together with the size of the target and its position relative to me, all are 'impressing' themselves upon my behaviour in respect of them, all are shaping up that behaviour into an act of propulsion of just the right force and angle, etc.

All action in respect of objects is motivated, it is moved by impulse. To the extent that the impulse determines the actual form of the action, to the extent that it shapes behaviour, action is *expressive* and it gives rise to 'feeling-form'. To the extent that the object in respect of which the individual is acting shapes his behaviour and not the impulse, action is impressive and it gives rise to 'object-form'.

We need now to formulate what has been said about expressive and impressive action in terms of the process that I have held to define all action, namely that of projection through a medium. When my action is expressive, it is my impulse (feeling-impulse) that is projected through the medium of objects whether these be physical or symbolic. Similarly when my action is impressive, it is the objects that are projected through the medium of my behaviour in respect of them. All action ranges along a continuum from the most purely expressive to the most purely impressive. To the extent that my actions in respect of objects receive the impression of those objects they constitute a '*medium of impression*' through which those objects are projected. To the extent that my actions in respect of objects express my sensate impulse, the disturbing of my being, to that extent the objects constitute a '*medium of expression*' through which my sensate impulse is projected.

The here-and-now and the there-and-then of action

Action consists of the inter-projection of a behavioural medium and its object medium. The media themselves, i.e. behaviour and object, are always in the present, in the here-and-now but that which is projected is always in the past, in the there-and-then. I press my finger into the clay. The clay registers the imprint of my finger at once and yet, as an event, the movement of my finger has already taken place at the instant that it is registered as an impression in the clay. Thus, as the projection through the medium (the clay) is taking place, what is projected (the movement of my finger) has already occurred. In the medium of the here-and-now I project that which is there-and-then. Similarly, as I depress my finger in the clay, the clay resists my finger in various ways thereby displacing my behaviour and causing me to alter the angle and force of depression. In the very instant of my finger movement registering the 'resistance' of the clay, that resistance has already occurred. In the medium of the here-and-now (the behaviour), I project that which is there-and-then (the resistance of the clay to my finger movements). The projection of a behavioural medium through its object medium is therefore the projection of the past of behaviour in the present of the object medium, and the projection of an object medium through its behavioural medium is the projection of the past of the object in the present of the behavioural medium.

It is here that we come to the basis of adaptive process and therefore of all action. Firstly, I can only become adapted in my environment to the extent that my behaviour can register (in becoming displaced) my past encounters with the world of objects. These encounters have already taken place by the time they are registered despite the fact that I *notice* no temporal gap between an encounter and its displacement of my behaviour. Secondly, I can only be adapted to the extent that the object medium registers my behaviour which is already past at the instant of its displacing elements in that medium. The instant between behaviour and projection or between object and projection is so short that it cannot be grasped as such in consciousness. The behaviour and its projection appear as one, in the present, as does the object and its projection. It is only by bringing the past and present together in this way that adaptation can take place. More specifically, the process of adaptation is a process of oscillating intensively between using the past of a behavioural medium to displace the present of its object medium, and using the past of that object medium to displace the present of its behavioural medium. The use of the terms 'past' and 'present' in relation to object and behaviour may appear a little strange at first, and so it will be as well to re-emphasize what is meant by them. Quite simply my behaviour is past when it has been 'impelled' (moved by impulse) and the object is past when it has been encountered by my behaviour. *After it has been impelled,* my behaviour is projected through its object medium. *After it has been encountered,* the object is projected through its behavioural medium.

The above analysis applies to subject response as well as object response. My encounters with the world of objects displace not only my behaviours in respect of objects but also my sensing in respect of objects which in turn engenders new behaviours in respect of objects. If my behaviour is controlled directly by the specific properties of the object then it is more purely impressive, whereas if it is controlled by my sensate impulse (subject response) then it is more purely expressive (all behaviour containing something at least of both elements). We can now picture the process diagrammatically as follows:

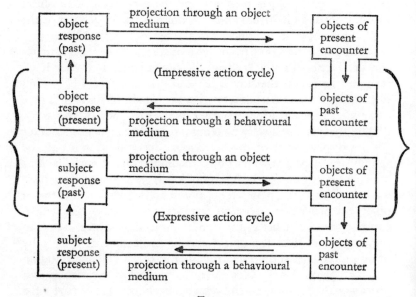

FIG. 1

In action, the past and the present are brought very close together, so close that I experience the past as the present. The fact that in action we cannot experience the hiatus between past and present ought not to blind us to the fact that there is such a hiatus and that all action is fundamentally reflective. It is a projection of the there-and-then of my experience in the here-and-now.

8

Knowing as action

In a sense, the terms 'knowing' and 'action' refer to one and the same process. They are the projection of an object medium through its behavioural medium and vice versa. This will become increasingly apparent as the analysis proceeds. On the other hand, there is some advantage in isolating 'knowing' as a rather special kind of action in that a large part of what we call 'knowing' is an intermediate stage of acting in the head prior to acting in the world. Certainly, the more abstract and symbolic 'knowing' becomes, the more completely does it constitute a distinct field of action, one that is relatively independent of the constraints of organising action in the real world. Symbolic knowing is action that is mobile, experimental and flexible in ways that sensory-motor action in the world could never be. Its function is to permit the organisation of behaviour and object to grow in complexity and elaboration to meet the adaptive demands made upon the individual in respect of them. In its more rudimentary forms, knowing is action restricted to sensory motor manipulation, whereas in its more advanced forms, it extends to operations upon symbols. The more advanced forms develop directly out of the more rudimentary forms, however, and there is no new functioning principle involved. Knowing, whether it is symbolic action or sensory-motor action is the interprojection of a behavioural medium and its object medium, bearing in mind of course that behaviour may be physical or mental and objects real or symbolic.

Knowing, therefore, subsumes behaviour that is expressive as well as behaviour that is impressive. Through his expressive behaviour the individual comes to know his sensing in respect of the world. His expressive behaviour projects his sensate impulse through an object medium. Through his impressive behaviour the individual comes to know the world in which he had his Being. Objects in the world are projected through the medium of his operations in respect of them. When knowing becomes symbolic action, then the media of impression and of expression make use of symbols in the head of the individual. For reasons that we shall note later, the use of the symbol permits the individual to produce extremely pure forms of impressive and expressive behaviour, of objectivity and subjectivity. Using symbols is simply a more mobile, flexible and efficient way of organising experience and thereby of making sense of the world and of one's Being in the world. Unless the individual can do this, action

9

(i.e. adapted behaviour) in the world is not possible. He must be able to organise the there-and-then of his experience in the here-and-now.

For the purpose of exploring our model more fully we will distinguish more sharply between knowing which is the result of impressive behaviour, i.e. the knowing of objects, and knowing which is the result of expressive behaviour i.e. the knowing of sensate impulse. The former we will refer to as *object-knowing* and the latter as *subject-knowing*. One important point must be made at the outset. Subject-knowing refers only to the knowing of my sensate impulse, of the disturbing of my Being in the world. It does not refer to the knowing of facts about myself, *that* I have inhibitions, *that* I am talkative, *that* I am reticent. Such facts about me belong to the same universe as facts about others and facts about objects. They are part of object-knowing.

Knowing, Self, and Being

At this point we need to elaborate upon our conception of the genesis of action before we deal more specifically with the processes of object-knowing and subject-knowing. I have argued that action consists in the interprojection of a behavioural medium and an object medium and that it is either 'impressive' or 'expressive' depending upon whether the object response is directly 'controlled' by the object or by the subject response. Furthermore, I have argued that knowing is simply a special form of action with no new fundamental principle involved. However, while it is true that all knowing is action, the converse is certainly not true. All action is not knowing. The purpose of this section is to locate knowing more specifically within the context of action as a whole and to tackle one or two theory problems concerning the nature of the 'knower' as such.

The distinction between expressive and impressive action made earlier concerned the relationship between that component of the individual's response which I termed 'object response' and either the subject response (sensate impulse) on the one hand, or the object, on the other. It was argued that where the shape or form of the individual's object response appeared to be determined by the specific characteristics of the object then the behaviour was impressive. Similarly, it was argued, that where the form or shape of the object response followed the impulse and was determined by it, the action was expressive. The object response may be symbolic or real, of course. It is the 'active' component of behaviour as distinct from the 'passive' and it is no less active for taking place in the head of the individual. Every response, has both this active and passive component, but the responses differ in the extent to which one or other component is dominant, and it is here that we obtain our distinction between impressive and expressive action. In impressive action, the object response is dominant whereas in expressive action it is the subject response that is dominant.

Nevertheless, the distinction between impressive action and expressive action will not suffice in itself. Both types include action that is knowing and action that is not. To pursue this problem of locating knowing within action generally, we need to introduce another distinction concerning the relationship between subject response and object response and between object and object response. Where the subject response is dominant it can control the object response in two senses. In the first sense it may simply release itself in an object response, i.e. the latter may be responsive to it. I feel happy so I release my joy by throwing my hat into the air. I feel angry so I kick the door, thereby releasing my anger in door kicking. In both of these examples there is a *reactive* relationship between the object response and the subject response which dominates it. I will therefore term this type of relationship *subject-reactive*. There is another type of reactive relationship which concerns behaviour in which the object response is dominant. In this case the reactive relationship exists between the object response and the object. When a soldier on a parade ground halts or jumps to attention when an order is given, his behaviour is reactive. Similarly when I cross the road and quicken my pace because the lights have suddenly changed, my behaviour is reactive. In both of these cases however, it is the situational requirement that controls my behaviour, i.e. releases it. Naturally, of course, such situational requirements are mediated through me, i.e. through my interpreting them, but it is the object that releases the behaviour once it has been encountered. I will therefore term this type of behaviour '*object-reactive*'.

In so far as my behaviour is reactive it evinces the property of *responsiveness*. This is one vital aspect of the adaptive process. If a man crosses the road with a firm purposeful step, it will avail him nothing if there are lights or vehicles that he does not see or hear.

If his behaviour is not responsive then he will be ill-adapted to the requirement of crossing the road. However, it is not sufficient to be simply responsive in order to meet the requirements of adaptation. To be fully adapted the individual's behaviour must be effective as well as responsive. If a man sees and hears everything but fails to move quickly enough to get out of the way of an oncoming car, then his behaviour, although responsive, is not effective. Whereas responsiveness comprises a reactivity between object response and subject response or between object response and object, effectiveness consists of a *reflexiveness* between them. Behaviour is reflexive to the extent that there is a reciprocal relationship between the object response and either the subject response or the object. By 'reciprocity' is meant here a relationship in which the object response is literally the counterpart of reciprocal of one of the other two. If I itch (subject response) and I then scratch (object response) my scratch may be said to be the counterpart of my itch. It is its reciprocal and will be effective in the sense of cancelling it out. My scratching behaviour is therefore '*subject-reflexive*'. It differs from subject-reactive behaviour in that in the case of the latter there is no reciprocity, no reciprocal relationship between the object response and the subject response. When I jump for joy, my jump cannot be said to be the reciprocal of my joy although it is most certainly an extension of it. Similarly my jump does not resolve my joy or cancel it out, although it may well use up all my energy.

The same type of reciprocity can occur in the relationship between the object response and an object. If I cup my hands to catch a ball there is an implicitness between my cupping action and the approaching ball. My cupping action is the counterpart, the reciprocal of the approaching ball. It is the action that will cancel or resolve the approaching ball. My cupping action is therefore *object-reflexive*. It differs from object-reactive behaviour in that in the latter case there is no reciprocity in the relationship of the object response to the object. There is no reciprocal cancelling out. When the soldier jumps to attention, or when I quicken my pace when the lights change, these actions are not the reciprocals of the objects that released them (the command of attention! and the traffic lights). The jumping to attention is merely an '*extension*' of the command. Similarly the change in the lights is extended in the change in my pace. Reactive behaviour always extends the subject response or object in the object response, but in reflexive behaviour the object response 'reciprocates' in some way. In reflexive behaviour there is some 'countering' of the object or subject response by the object response. The latter serves as a counterpart or reciprocal.

This reciprocity that is the basis for reflexive action may be only partial. To that extent, action itself is only partially reflexive. The fact is that all four components (subject and object reflexiveness and subject and object reactiveness) are present in all behaviour in some combination but behaviours vary considerably in the extent to which one or another component is dominant. A closer look at the examples I have given above should reveal this. In the case of re-active behaviour the subject response or the object is extended in the object response. Nevertheless this extension must meet some kind of resistance. This resistance, which is always there in some degree is a form of reciprocity. It is a reflexiveness implicit in every piece of reactive behaviour. The officer's command cannot be perfectly extended in the recruit's behaviour. The recruit's behaviour in responding will resist the command to the extent of the limitations of 'reflexes' and physical capabilities at least. Such resistance may be insignificant from the point of view of either party, but it exists as a tiny component of reflexiveness in this basically reactive form of behaviour. Absolute responsiveness in a recruit would be a phy-sical impossibility although something approaching it may be achieved. Since there is always resistance to behaviour, there is always reflexiveness, however minute a component it may be. Similarly there would be no point in jumping for joy if it were not for the fact that what goes up must come down. The jump is not a perfect extension of the joyous impulse. It embodies some resist-ance and therefore some reflexiveness. In a fully reflexive act the resistance to the object or the subject response is built into the object response to the extent of being fully reciprocal. Nevertheless, there is always a reactive component, no matter how insignificant, in reflexive behaviour. Just as resistance is never absent from behaviour, so it is never absolute. Absolute reflexiveness is an impossibility since there will always be some minute amount of the object response that will not reciprocate the subject response or object. This minute amount will comprise an extension of either subject response or object. It will therefore be a reactive component. If I scratch in response to my itch then to the extent that there is some small part of the scratch that is not used up in dispelling the itch, that part is a subject-reactive component. Similarly, in cupping my hands to catch the approaching ball there will be some small part of my response that is not part of the catching of the ball. That part is an object-reactive component. Absolute reflexiveness or absolute reactiveness is an impossibility simply because all action consists in the interprojection of two media, behavioural and object (symbolic or real). Each medium is a source of resistance for the other and to that extent resistance must vary in any behaviour along a continuum ranging from the minute to the considerable and not from zero to the absolute.

Before going on to say something about the differentiation of behaviour with respect to the four components, it might be helpful to consider them in their relatively undifferentiated state in the simple reflex. One such reflex that we can consider is the eyeblink response to a puff of air. The eyeblink reciprocates both the smarting of the eye (subject-reflexive) and the puff of air (object-reflexive). It is a self-contained little parcel of adapted behaviour. Nevertheless, it is extremely inflexible in so far as it is simply engaged again and again using itself up completely each time and not incorporating itself as experience in some structure. In order for such an incorporative structure to emerge, the reflexiveness, i.e., the reciprocation, must occur in a medium that is different from the subject response or the object that releases it. The easiest difference to conceive of here is that between the physical world and the symbolic. If the reflexiveness of my response to a physical object is constituted on a symbolic level then it is not used up on the object. It persists as a reciprocal action that has not been cancelled out. If my response to thirst is simply to drink then my drinking reciprocates my thirst but the two cancel each other out in the process. If my response to my thirst is to picture water then this is a reciprocal that is not cancelled out by my thirst. The use of reciprocals that are not cancelled out in the process of being activated, simply because they occur on a different level of operation from that of the subject response or object that gives rise to them, is the basis of all knowing. *Action that is knowing is action that is reflexive between two levels of operation, the most obvious illustration being that of reflexive action between the physical and the symbolic levels of operation.*

When action is reflexive between two levels of operation, it begins to incorporate itself. That is, the reciprocals that are produced become integrated with one another in a reflexive core or structure. If we remain with our distinction between the physical and the symbolic, the process can be described as follows: If action is subject-reflexive then a disturbance which arises within the individual (subject response) gives rise to a subject-reflexive response on a symbolic level which is then incorporated into a structure of such responses that have been built up in the past. Similarly, if action is object-reflexive then the object gives rise to an object-reflexive response on a symbolic level which is then incorporated into a structure of such responses that have been built up in the past. The structure, or core of reflexive response is therefore continually transformed by new reflexive acts.

We are now in a position to say something about that most mysterious character, the 'knower'. Here I will take a decidedly non-mystical approach to the problem. In awareness, the individual manifests a unified presence. I will argue that it is profitable to conceive of this presence as that same integrated core of reflexive response built up over time, of which I have been speaking. The knower may thus be conceived of purely as a core of reflexive response. Furthermore we can conceive of this core as being in two parts, an inner core and an outer core. The inner core consists of subject-reflexive response and the outer core of object-reflexive response. The former I shall term Being and the latter the self.

These two structures, Being and the self, mediate all knowing. Sensation is experienced in Being as disturbance (sensate impulse). This sensate impulse is then expressed in a reciprocal (a subject-reflexive symbolic act) which is incorporated into Being. The sensation does not originate in Being but from outside Being. It disturbs Being which then responds reflexively (on a symbolic level). The disturbance is literally known-in-being when the reflexive response is incorporated. The same process occurs in the case of the self. The object exists beyond the self. In this case, the self encounters the object and the latter is impressed in a reciprocal (an object-reflexive symbolic act) which is then integrated into the self. Both self and Being are the fabric of awareness. They are the knower.

The knower is thus continually transformed by new reflexive acts, new knowing. Through these transformations he transcends his relationships with both objects and his own sensate experience. It is this possibility of continuous transformation of self and Being that adds an entirely new dimension to the adaptive process in the case of man. It is man's self that acts in the world, and his Being that is disturbed in the world. When Being and self are reactive they are merely extended (and expended) in the world and there is no transformation in them. The growth of Being and self requires reflexive action between two levels of operation, it requires knowing.

The advantage of adopting this conceptualisation is that it does not violate the psychological level of analysis. Being and self are quite simply identified with the organised structure of reflexive response that is developed by the individual in his acts of reciprocating events on one level of operation in another level of operation. We can picture the process in the following way (see Fig. 2).

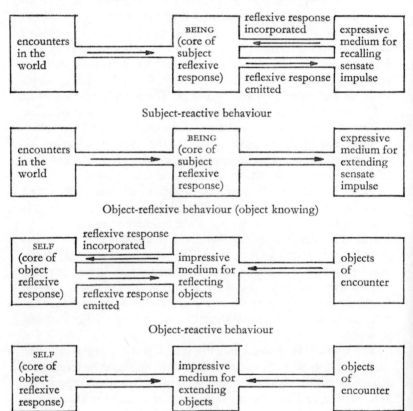

FIG. 2

With increasing complexity in the adaptive problem there is a growing division of labour between the components of action (subject and object reflexiveness and reactiveness). Extremely pure forms emerge that are integrated in larger action systems. The process of creative science constitutes one of the purer forms of object-reflexive action and that of the creative arts one of the purer forms of subject-reflexive action. Since it is the reflexive component of action that concerns me most in this work will examine these two forms of action in more detail.

Object-knowing (object-reflexive action)

If I pick up a stone and weigh it in the palm of my hand, press it with my thumb, run my fingers lightly across its surface, feel its contours, throw it in the air, rub it and squeeze it, I can abstract the properties of the stone in respect of my weighing, rubbing, squeezing, throwing, etc. The stone is hard, smooth, irregular in shape. It resists being depressed by my thumb or being squeezed, etc. The developmental psychology of Jean Piaget is rich in illustrations of operations like these performed by infants and young children as part of the process of coming to grips with the world of objects, of coming to know objects. In the example just given the stone is known by me as those operations of mine that it facilitates as distinct from those that it does not, as what I can do in respect of it as distinct from what I cannot do, e.g. it is throwable and hard, it resists being treated as malleable or regular in shape. My operations upon the stone are effected by the specific properties of the stone. More precisely the results of my operations are registered in the tailoring or 'shaping up' of those same operations upon the stone until the stone can be completely apprehended by them. In operating upon the stone my own operations are displaced as they encounter the specific properties of the stone. These displacements constitute a progressive refinement, a shaping up of my operations, until they cohere as a mould for the stone, *an action mould, one that registers the specific properties of the stone as action in respect of it. The stone as an object exists for me as my articulated actions in respect of it.*

This example of manipulating the stone deals with the knowing of objects at a fairly rudimentary level in that knowledge is abstracted from the object itself. There is a level of knowing immediately above this in which knowledge is not abstracted directly from operating upon the object but from operating upon an operation upon the

object. One of the finest illustrations of this is given by Jean Piaget (*Genetic Epistemology*) when he recalls what a mathematician acquaintance of his told him of his childhood discovery of the wonder of number. I will render the account somewhat freely. The child takes ten stones and arranges them in a circle and then counts them going around the circle clockwise. He re-counts them going around the circle anticlockwise. He then arranges the same stones in a triangle and in a straight line, counting them each time and always obtaining the same result, the stones numbering ten. No matter how he arranges them they number ten and he is filled with wonder at his discovery. What seems so obvious to the adult and the older child is utterly remarkable to him. He has discovered that altering the spacial distribution of the stones in no way affects their number whereas hitherto he had always assumed, along with all children who have not yet reached this stage in their development, that the number of objects was altered when their distribution in space was changed. There are now numerous recorded experiments that demonstrate this primitive assumption on the part of young children. The important point, however, is that the child has not obtained this information from the stones themselves. It is nothing to do with their being smooth, hard, irregular in shape, etc. He has obtained the information by counting the stones in his different arrangements of the stones. Since it is the equivalence of the *arrangements* of the stones with respect to his *counting* of the stones that is known, he is in fact using one operation as a medium for the projection of the other, therefore, what is known, i.e. what is projected through a medium, is not the object but an operation upon the object. It is the arrangements of the stones projected through the counting operation in respect of them, and not the stones themselves. Projecting the arrangements of the stones through the medium of the counting operation in respect of them has the effect of displacing the counting operations in the same way. The counting operations remain undifferentiated from one another with respect to the differing arrangements. The stones are known as ten in number through all arrangings of them.

Although the child's operations in the above illustration remove him one level from the direct knowing of the object, both operations are themselves still in contact with the object. The operations consist of the child's *arrangings of the stones* and his *counting of the stones*. The child is still operating at a level which we will equate with Piaget's 'concrete operations'. At a still higher level of knowing the individual operates at more than one stage removed from the object, i.e. at a level in which the operations are not in contact with the object at all. We will equate this level with Piaget's stage of 'formal (symbolic) operations'. This latter level is an achievement of adolescent development. Knowing thus becomes progressively more symbolic and abstract. Nevertheless, the fundamental principle remains the same. The knowing of objects, real or symbolic, involves their projection through a medium comprising operations in respect of them, a medium of impression, through which the specific properties of the external world are apprehended in actions displaced by them.

Subject-knowing (subject-reflexive action)

The knowing of fact and object, vital though it is for the adaptation of the individual in his environment, is nevertheless quite insufficient in itself. To be properly adapted the individual requires to be able to relate meaningfully to the world in which he has his being. Without such personally meaningful relationships he would lack the motivation, the energy to move in the world at all. A vital part of the process of knowing, therefore involves the knowing of one's Being in the world, the knowing of one's sensing and feeling. This is really one of the most neglected and confused areas within epistemology. The problem hardly arises in Piaget's genetic epistemology because his basic assumptions about 'knowing' limit the process to what in our terms is subsumed by object-knowing. The cracks in the Piagetian framework appear when we begin to ask questions about the motivation of the child or the function of the mental image. Piaget's own accounts of both remain vague and unconvincing. No attempt will be made here to criticise the basic epistemological assumptions of Piagetian theory. The important point is not that I disagree with Piaget but that I am only able to do so because Piaget's framework contains within it the means of extending genetic epistemology into subject-knowing, and thereby the means of transforming his framework in the process.

There is a very great difficulty, however, in being able to discourse about subject-knowing without resorting to various kinds of technical circumlocution. This is because our consciousness is not yet adequately prepared to make the fundamental distinctions necessary to conceive of an intelligence of feeling. Such an idea appeals on an intuitive level but it resists thought to the extent that the subjective life as 'Being' lacks a proper language in which to talk about it. It is not a language to talk about feelings as such that we lack, but a language to talk about the process of feeling. We need to be able to grasp the epistemological significance of feeling its importance as a mode of knowing.

The most difficult prejudice to overcome is that which identifies sensation with knowing. This is in spite of the fact that Sigmund Freud founded an entire school of psychology upon the notion of the 'unconscious'. Most people, if they accept the idea that part of their deep experience remains unconscious, see in the 'unconscious' a locked chest full of ideas, desires, and other bits and pieces of forgotten self. This tends to obscure a general property of all sensation from my point of view, namely that *all* sensation is in itself 'unconscious', or 'unknowing'. The problem is not to ask why we come to know some of our sensing and to lock up the rest. It is rather to ask the general epistemological question of how we come to know any of our sensing at all.

We speak of 'pin-prick sensations' and 'butterflies in the stomach', of 'tingling in the spine' and so forth. Every description of sensation is really a reference to some specific property of the object world in respect of which the sensation may be evoked. They are not real butterflies that cause 'butterflies in the stomach' but 'butterflies in the stomach' is a phrase that describes the sensation of being 'all of a flutter inside'. It expresses the sensation through the (symbolic) medium of creatures that might evoke such a sensation in my stomach if they were fluttering about inside it. As soon as I consider some sensation that I have experienced it is already known by me. What is more important from our point of view, however, is that it is known by me in terms of some property of the object world through which it may be evoked (The reader is reminded here that the object world in our definition includes everything that is other than my sensate impulse. It even includes 'me' in so far as 'me' can be taken as an object.) The simple answer to the question of how we come to know any of our sensing is that we only know it in so far as we *express* our sensing in displacements in the object world, in so far as we project it in an 'object medium'. Sensing known is sensing expressed. It is sensing projected through the medium of that which evokes sensing, through the medium of the object.

To appreciate the basically unknowing character of sensation it has to be recognised that the experience of disturbance is not synonymous with knowing the disturbance. When sensation is evoked within the individual it is encountered by the inner core or structure of reflexive response that I have called Being. It is experienced as disturbance, as sensation, mood or emotionality depending upon the intensity, diffusion, and speed of build up of disturbance. Present awareness consists of the activation of the core of reflexive response that I have termed Being and Self. To say that sensation is encountered as a disturbance of Being is therefore synonymous with saying that it is encountered as a disturbance in present awareness. The sensation and Being, however, are on two different levels of operation. For the sensation to be known-in-Being, Being must express it in a subject-reflexive act which recalls it. It is this subject-reflexive act that is incorporated into Being. The reciprocal of the sensation is quite simply the (symbolic) reciprocal that recalls it. Expressive acts that recall the sensate experience are just such reciprocals. They resolve the disturbance of Being by reciprocating it on the level of Being. The reciprocal is thereby incorporated in Being. The reciprocation of a sensate impulse (subject response) is a *feeling-idea* just as the reciprocation of an object is a *concept*. Being is made up of feeling-idea. It has an order and a logic of its own. The structured and adaptive characteristics of Being are what is meant here by an intelligence of feeling. Feeling is quite distinct from mood or emotion. It is the reflexive component of the affective life. It is the fabric of Being. Mood and emotion are simply disturbance unknowing.

Of central importance in subject-knowing is the concept of *recall*. The expressing of a sensation 'recalls' that sensation. Let us return to the illustration of a child manipulating a stone. Let us assume for a moment that he is not interested in the stone as such but is 'absentmindedly' handling it with his fingers and, as it happens, his thumb lightly traverses its surface. Let us assume further that this yields a rough sensation with a smooth bump in the middle of it but it is gone before he is aware of it although he has noticed it. It exists as sensate impulse as yet unknown. The sensate impulse then drives the child to repeat the operation but the sensation is not recalled for his thumb is traversing a somewhat different area of the stone. He repeats it again and again and finally the sensation is recalled, only this time, in his active traversing of the surface of the stone, he knows his sensing of the stone. His sensing of the stone is thus expressed in his displacing of the medium of the stone (actively traversing its surface) and the displacement achieves its result when the sensate impulse which gave rise to his displacement of the stone is *recalled*. In subject-knowing the sensate impulse gives rise to the displacement of an expressive medium which recalls the sensing. The point is of crucial importance to us here because if my view is correct then this is the epistemological foundation of all the creative arts. I come to know the disturbing of my Being by recalling the disturbing of my Being. This recalling is facilitated by expression, by the displacement of an expressive medium.

Piaget records many instances in which an infant performs some action in respect of an object accidentally, e.g. he scratches it or pushes it with his fist, and because it produces a result which pleases him he then repeats this action in respect of all sorts of other objects as well as this one. Piaget terms this behaviour a circular reaction and attaches great adaptive significance to it. However, he treats of such circular reactions as though their adaptive value lay purely in their possibilities for knowing objects. They provide the child with new operations to perform on a wide range of objects. This almost certainly is an important function of such circular reactions but it is just as likely that an equally important function of circular reactions is that they enable the infant to know his sensing in respect of the object. In repeating the operation he is really recalling the sensation, i.e. expressing his sensing in order to know it. In so doing, however, he encounters new sensations in new objects and these feed the circular reaction in so far as he seeks to recall these too in his operations upon the object. Even in infancy we can find the embryonic forms of expressive action in the attempts made by the infant to know his sensing of the object as distinct from his attempt to know the object in respect of which he is sensing.

In subject-knowing the behaviour of the individual is shaped by the inner movement of sensate impulse which is projected through the expressive medium. In order to control the development of form in the expressive act, however, the consciousness of the individual must 'oscillate' intensively between the impulse and the medium. Only in this way can the impulse (which in itself is blind) be guided by its effect in the medium. This oscillation of the individual's consciousness between the sensate impulse and its effect in the medium sets up a guidance system for the impulse so that the latter can continually adjust expressive behaviour to the requirement of recalling sensing and thereby releasing the impulse. It is this oscillation which is the basis of reflexive control. It is the to-and-from movement whereby a sensate impulse is brought together with its effect upon the expressive medium in the ongoing creative process, and is thereby enabled to make the continuous fine adjustments in expressive behaviour required to realise feeling and release the impulse. When the individual's impulse moves through the medium of sound, when he composes a melody, his conscious-ness must oscillate between his impulse and the sound he is making. He must be able to bring the two together if he is to have any hope of his impulse shaping sounds in ways that will recall the sensing that gave rise to it.

The oscillation between impulse and medium can be likened to a sonar signalling system. The pulse probes the medium and the re-turning signal with its specific characteristics serves to guide further probes. This process continues intensively until outgoing probe and incoming signal are assimilated to one another, are the very echo of one another. By oscillating intensively between impulse and medium, the individual's consciousness brings the two pulses (outgoing and incoming) together. This sets up a 'reverberation' between them which modifies the next probe and so the process continues. The important point is that it is always reflexive. The individual always 'feels' his way through from start to finish. His sensing is at work upon the medium and reflected back from the medium. Sensing is always in control, shaping form for recall.

This oscillation between impulse and medium is further compli-cated by the fact that the form in progress interacts with the Being of the individual thereby creating new disturbance, new sensate impulse that enters into the reverberative process. The individual recalls sensing by creating form but in doing so new chords of sensate experience are plucked within him by his form-in-progress and these in turn give rise to expressive activity to recall them in form, which then plucks more chords of sensate experience and so on. The reverberation ceases when it is arbitrarily interfered with or when it has run its natural course through the sensate possibilities of the individual's Being. The artist remains unsatisfied to the ex-tent that the reverberation of his expressive form with both sensate impulse and Being is still in progress when the physical work must be brought to an end. In other words, there is some sensate impulse that is not 'reciprocated' if the reverberation has not run its full course. The intensive oscillation between impulse and medium therefore has two aspects. It both recalls sensate impulse and deepens and enlarges it in the process. In this way the sensate impulse that starts the creative act is itself modified in the very process of being recalled.

Just as in the most rudimentary forms of object-knowing, where the individual's operations are closely bound to the objects themselves, so in rudimentary subject-knowing they are equally bound in that the medium in which sensing is directly expressed consists often of the same objects which gave rise to the sensing. Again, as with object-knowing, the more advanced modes are progressively more abstract and symbolic, becoming increasingly independent of the specific objects that provoke the sensing. They become *sensings in respect of sensings*, as a counterpart to the *operations in respect of operations* in object-knowing. It is also the case that the closer one is to experiencing the object itself the more difficult it is to differentiate subject-knowing from object-knowing. This is because the same actions serve both an expressive and impressive function as in the case of the infant's 'circular reaction' described above. Using symbols permits one to bring about a great separation between acts of impression and acts of expression.

The creative artist works at very high levels of symbolic action. Disturbance is evoked within him and is experienced as sensate impulse. This sensate impulse guides his expressive act in the symbolic medium. The expressive action itself is the reciprocal (subject-reflexive) of the disturbance within him and what is recalled as a result is the disturbance (sensate impulse). It is recalled through the medium of that which will evoke it. The only creative act given to man is the act of reciprocation.

Media of impression

In the account of object-knowing, a 'medium of impression' was described as consisting of the operations that an individual performs upon an object and through which that object is projected. Thus in operating upon the stone my operations were displaced in various ways as the specific properties of the stone impressed themselves upon them. My operations thus constituted a medium of impression.

The most important characteristic of such a medium is that the operations of which it consists should be as independent as possible of the direct sensing of the object. If the individual's direct sensing of the object in part determines these operations, to that extent the operations themselves cannot be free to receive the impression of the object. In other words if the operations upon the object are under the control of the individual's direct sensing of the object then they will be expressive rather than impressive. Ideally, an impressive medium is one which offers no facility to the expression of the individual's sensate impulse.

At the most rudimentary levels of knowing, impressive and expressive operations are closely identified with one another. I may rub the stone both to know my sensing of the stone and to know the stone in respect of which I am sensing. Is my operation of rubbing the stone therefore part of a medium of impression or is it an expressive operation? The answer is that it may be either, depending upon how my consciousness uses the operation. On all levels of knowing the operations of impression and those of expression may be differentiated from one another according to the way in which they are used in consciousness.

Even though there is some distinction between expressive and impressive operations on all levels of knowing, it is certainly true that on the more rudimentary levels of knowing, where one and the same operation may serve both an expressive and an impressive function, the medium of impression is far from ideal. Later on, as the child comes increasingly to perform operations in his head making use of symbolic representation, the operations of impression diverge more widely from those of expression. The power of representation permits the individual operating on a symbolic level to differentiate much more clearly between media of impression and media of expression simply because he can construct such media of symbols that have a purely expressive function and symbols that have a purely impressive function in addition to being able to make use of symbols that can be used in either context as expressive or impressive.

I have already argued that the most ideal medium of impression is one in which the operations of impression are as free as possible of the control of the individual's direct sensing. Such a medium will not register the direct sensing of the object but will be responsive to the 'impression' of the object qua object. The languages of logic and algebra provide clear examples of such symbol media. Mathematical symbols can be used to represent the world of objects without embodying any of the sensate possibilities of the objects themselves and, therefore, without providing any possibilities for the expressions of the individual's sensate impulses in respect of the objects represented. A world of objects, represented by x's and y's might just as well be represented by b's and z's. There is no necessary connection between the symbols and what they refer to. The connection is purely and deliberately arbitrary. x's and y's are impervious to the sensory possibilities of the world of objects that they represent. As such they constitute a relatively pure medium of impression. Through such a medium of symbolic operations, the properties of the object qua object, independent of the sensory properties of the object, can be projected, can be known.

While the languages of the sciences, logic and mathematics constitute relatively pure media of impression, natural language may be said to have a dual function. Words, as the basic meaningful elements in natural languages, are rather like symbols in mathematics and logic in that they bear, with certain exceptions, an arbitrary relationship to their referents. There is no necessary connection between the words 'apple pie' and the apple-pie-experience. Different words could be used to represent the same experience in different languages. The word, like the logic-algebraical symbol, is used to represent the object without incorporating within itself any of the sensory stimulus properties of the apple pie. The apple pie is therefore able to exist for us as an object in its own right without becoming confused in consciousness with our sensing of it. There is nothing *in the word itself* which is 'apple-pieish'. A word, therefore is basically a discursive symbol and it shares this property in common with other discursive symbols such as those of logico-algebraical discourse. Natural language differs from logico-algebracial discourse, however, in that words, when used in combination may be made to serve either an impressive or an expressive function. In referential discourse they clearly serve an impressive function whereas in poetry they serve an expressive function. We will not concern ourselves here with the question of how this is possible but merely point out that the dual function of words with respect to object- and subject-knowing gives them a flexibility and a range of usage far greater than that of either a pure medium of impression or a pure medium of expression.

Media of expression

I have stated that the ideal medium of impression is one in which the operations upon the object that constitute it are as unaffected by the individual's direct sensing of the object as possible. On a symbolic level of operation this is achieved by making use of symbols that bear an arbitrary relationship to their referents such as words or mathematical symbols. A medium of expression, on the other hand, is the exact opposite of this. It consists either of objects that have the power of evoking direct sensate experience, or of representations on a symbolic level that incorporate the direct sensate possibilities of objects. Thus media of expression always have the power of stimulating directly. When the individual then displaces such media in response to his sensing he is able to recall his sensing. The ideal medium of expression, is therefore one which 'simulates' the stimulus properties of objects in a way that is as independent of the apprehending of the object qua object as is possible. Such media we will refer to as *iconic* and we will contrast them with *discursive* media. There are problems with the term 'iconic' however in that it has connotations that are strongly dominated by the visual media of stimulation. One tends to think in terms of 'pictures' when one speaks of iconic representation. We will explicitly reject this restriction and use the term 'iconic' to refer to any symbolic emulation of the sensory stimulus properties of objects whether such emulation be auditory, visual, tactile or whatever. It is true, however, that iconic representation tends to be dominated by the visual mode, in the same way that discursive representation tends to be dominated by natural language. Words, it was argued, bear an arbitrary relationship to the stimulus properties of the objects to which they refer but in combination they can be made to serve either an expressive function, as in poetry, or an impressive function, as in factual discourse. Visual icons on the other hand actually emulate the stimulus properties of the object world but again, in combination, they can be made to serve either an expressive function, as in the visual arts, or an impressive function, as in the veridical perception of objects. Visual iconic representation is therefore the counterpart of natural language in that it can serve a dual function both as a medium of impression and as a medium of expression. In a sense the auditory iconic modes of representation are the purest because they are highly flexible in their capacity to emulate the stimulus properties of the object world without apprehending objects as such. Thus when people refer to music as the most abstract of all the arts they are really responding to this capacity of the auditory medium to permit the abstraction of the sensory properties of the object world from the objects in which they are embedded. Music is really the counterpart of mathematical and logical languages. Whereas they abstract the object independent of its sensate possibilities and they achieve this more completely than words, music abstracts the sensate possibilities independent of the objects in which they are embedded and it achieves this more completely than visual ikons. All expressive media, however, are media of direct stimulation and they are most purely expressive when they are impervious to the properties of the object qua object. The dominance of the word and the visual icon as modes of representation may well derive from their capacity to do what neither the purely expressive nor the purely impressive media can do, namely to provide a subtle harmony and blending of subject and object in a single form.

The motivational problem

To be adapted in his environment the individual must be able to act effectively as an integrated person. This involves managing the world as object and himself as object within it on the one hand, and on the other, managing the disturbance evoked within him as a consequence of his Being in the world. In the former context the person can be conceived of as a self-in-action and in the latter context as a Being-in-action. Action in the world is thus double-edged. It must be effective as a system for the organising of object relations and at the same time it must be effective in releasing the sensate disturbance that builds within the individual and which energises his behaviour. If the demands made upon the individual in respect of object relations and action in the world are quite disjunctive with the demands made upon the individual by the disturbance evoked within him then the integration between Being and self will break down. This condition of disjunction between Being and self is often referred to as 'alienation', literally the state of Being estranged from oneself. Action in the world becomes increasingly difficult as the individual succumbs to a motivational crisis in which he finds himself either with behaviour for which he has no impulse, or impulse for which he has no behaviour.

There are many in our schools and universities who have lost the ground between Being and self. The anxiety of those who love them to see them successful in object management is the Trojan horse that has breached the citadel to the person. Retreatism abounds. Existence comes to depend upon it. Then there are those for whom there is little concern, who feel constantly threatened, and for whom object management is not even a possibility. In these 'rejects' a deep subject-reactive violence simmers and boils. Not for them the enervated routines of the Being in retreat. Theirs is the cyclical repetition of charge and discharge.

The world in which our educational system has developed has made immense demands upon it to mould its charges in the image of rationality and the objective standpoint. The tremendous forces unleashed in the productive enterprise of the twentieth century have appeared to require as much from society's operations. This process cannot continue indefinitely. Man as object, as self, has grown through object-reflexive action at the expense of man as subject, as Being. To overcome the disjunction, man as Being must grow. Education must rediscover a real concern with subject-reflexive action. Subject-reflexive action is the foundation of an intelligence of feeling. It is the process whereby Being is transformed and thereby transcends its former relationship to the world.

2 From Beyond the Expressive Act

In the first chapter the intelligence of feeling was identified as the organised process of subject-reflexive action. The creative arts provide instances of highly developed uses of subject-reflexive action. They stand in relation to the intelligence of feeling as the sciences do to logical reasoning. The failure to develop arts curricula in schools systematically and to give a priority to subject-reflexive action and its development which is in line with its vital importance in the adaptive process, will almost certainly have to be overcome if schools are to meet the adaptational requirements of the future.

In this chapter the theoretical framework outlined so far will undergo further development and elaboration within the specific context of the teaching of the creative arts. The framework will be literally 'worked through' the teaching process itself in an attempt to reveal the logic that underlies the arts teacher's praxis. In Part Two, the framework will be worked through a series of empirical encounters with this praxis in schools. The term praxis, as used here, subsumes both the practice of teachers, what they do, together with their consciousness in respect of what they do. In terms of my method, the concept of working the framework through the praxis of teachers is a central one. The theoeretical framework is not an explanation which I attach to teaching nor is it a prescription. Rather it is a frame of reference for looking at knowing within the general context of action and for differentiating between types of knowing within that context. To develop the framework as substantive theory with respect to teaching, it is necessary to work it through the praxis of teachers, in the first instance to uncover the logic implicit in that praxis and then to illustrate and fill out this logic with empirical instance. Only when the theoretical framework has been used to expose the logic and meaning of praxis will there be a real basis for a substantive theory of curriculum development, one which will serve to guide the current phase in the evolution of curricula. While it is true that this chapter will concern itself specifically with the logic and not with the empirical content of praxis, it is also true that an analysis of the logic presupposes some empirical encounter with the content. Both this chapter and Part Two make use of the same empirical encounters; the distinction between them rests in the way these encounters are used. In this chapter the logic of the encounters is abstracted from the empirical content to a considerable extent in order to provide a basis for comprehending the meaning of the teacher's praxis. In Part Two the content of the teacher's praxis is used both to illustrate and fill out this logic. To the extent that this can be done comprehensively we have the basis for formulating a substantive theoretical approach to curriculum development in the creative arts. The test of such a theory rests with the future praxis of teachers. Thus the theory which emerges from an analysis-in-praxis can only be tested in future praxis. There are those who would say that such a method is unscientific, arguing that if one formulates a theory of meaningful action, and people then behave in accordance with that theory, the theory is not thereby tested by their behaviour. On the contrary, such critics would argue, the theory is simply a 'self-fulfilling prophecy' and people only behave that way because they have been persuaded to believe it. I shall not argue this issue here but merely assert that I disagree entirely with such a point of view. It presumes that the individual is able to make use of any plausible account of action in determining his praxis. I believe this notion reflects an unsound view of the relationship between consciousness and practice. No matter what rationalisation of his action the individual accepts in the short term, the only one that will work effectively for him, is that rationale which has comprehended the real logical basis of his praxis. A false rationalisation of the individual's praxis shows up in praxis itself as breakdown or crisis. It is in this sense that I believe that the real test of an analysis-in-praxis is the praxis that emerges as a consequence of the analysis.

In identifying the common epistemological root of all the different creative arts as that of being subject-reflexive action, we have a basis for unifying our approach and for making statements that are as applicable to music and dance as they are to sculpture or creative writing. In order to work this framework through the praxis of teachers and abstract its logic I will establish a number of categories in terms of which that praxis can be comprehended. These are derived directly from a consideration of the consciousness of teachers. The framework can thereby enter the praxis of teachers, not simply in its own terms, but through the consciousness of teachers.

The most central category is that of *'self-expression and individuality'*. The idea that the creative arts afford a real opportunity for self-expression and the individual approach to a greater extent than do other parts of the curriculum, and that they are about the individual and his personal relating to the world rather than about facts, is deep in the consciousness of arts teachers. Equally deep, however, is the teacher's concern with the effectiveness that the pupil achieves in expressive acts as determined by his success or otherwise in managing the medium in which his expressive acts take place. *'Control of the medium'* is therefore the second of our categories. The creative act has significance not only from the point of view of one's own production of an expressive form but also from the point of view of the utilisation of expressive forms produced by others. The expressive forms of others are used in different contexts. The individual may relate to them (in appreciation) as part of the process of subject-knowing, i.e. as the basis for subject-reflexive action in a purely individual context. On the other hand he may use expressive form as part of a process of critical evaluation, or he may use it in the context of an interpretative act, as in the playing of a piece of music or the enactment of a play. He may also use it as an expressive landmark in relation to his own expressive action. All of these instances are summed up in our third category, *'the use of realised form'*. The notion that the child's self-expression reveals his personal and social maturity, is also very deep in the consciousness of arts teachers. Our fourth category will therefore be *personal development*. Finally, the arts teacher participates with other teachers in a deep concern with the process by which progress on the part of both teacher and pupil can be assessed and the part that examinations play in this. Our fifth category will therefore be *examinations and assessment*. In themselves these categories enable us to do no more than list the practices of arts teachers in a way that reflects the preoccupations of arts teachers. The logic of praxis is not revealed until the theoretical framework enters the categories and is worked through them.

1 Self-expression and individuality

While the teacher of the creative arts regards self-expression as fundamental, his understandng of self-expression embraces a number of disparate activities which forces him to recognise only some forms of expressive action as legitimate while viewing others as quite illegitimate. This distinction between legitimate and illegitimate forms of self-expression is forced upon the teacher because of his failure to make a more fundamental distinction, such as the one that I made earlier, between subject-reactive and subject-reflexive behaviour and to perceive the nature of the relationship between the latter and the production of expressive form. Thus an individual is said to be expressing himself, albeit in a wholly illegitimate way, when he kicks in a window pane or daubs a lavatory wall, just as surely as he is held to be expressing himself (in a legitimate way) when he paints a picture or composes a piece of music. The kicking in of a window in response to an angry impulse is in my terms an example of 'subject-reactive' behaviour. The individual extends the sensate impulse, the disturbance within him, in behaviour in a medium. The impulse is released and burned up in the behaviour but the behaviour does not reciprocate it. The behaviour is not a means of recalling the disturbance and thereby of assimilating it into Being. In subject-reactive behaviour a disturbance is discharged without being assimilated into Being. When the individual paints a picture or composes a piece of music, however, his use of the expressive medium reciprocates his impulse in the sense of being that which recalls it. Such behaviour, if it does reciprocate in this way, is 'subject-reflexive'.

At first sight it would appear that the distinction which I have made between subject-reactive and subject-reflexive behaviour corresponds to the distinction which the teacher may make in his own terms between self-expression that is legitimate and self-expression that is not. This is misleading, however. The distinction between legitimate and non-legitimate forms of self-expression is made by the teacher on the basis of a consideration of the implications and consequences of the behaviour in some social frame of reference. It has nothing to do with differentiating between behaviours in terms of their intrinsic character as action and knowing. In other words, in making the distinction between legitimate and non-legitimate expressive acts there is no impli-

33

cation that the teacher comprehends any difference in the epistemological status of the acts that he has contrasted. His distinction
is an *evaluative* one which says nothing of a real intrinsic difference between the acts themselves.

The failure to distinguish reactive from reflexive behaviour on
an intrinsic level has profound consequences for the praxis of
teachers. In the absence of intrinsic criteria to comprehend differences between expressive acts, the teacher is obliged to fall back on
the extrinsic and frequently irrelevant criteria upon which the
distinction between the legitimate and non-legitimate is built. The
common element in all expressive acts that the teacher is able to
detect is the fact that all such acts release sensate impulse. In
abstracting what appears to him to be the common element in a
highly disparate range of activities, the teacher easily alights upon
the notion of 'catharsis'. Self-expression is said to have a cathartic
effect in that it is a means for releasing sensate impulse, for discharg-
ing tensions, for getting one's feelings into some sort of external
form. This identifying of the common element of self-expressive
acts as being the cathartic release engenders a wholly ambivalent
attitude in teachers with respect to self-expression. The discharge
of impulse alone is something that I have held to be characteristic
of subject-reactive behaviour. The teacher therefore perceives in
self-expression both a positive necessity and a disturbing threat.
He sees it as both creative and constructive on the one hand and as
destructive and anarchical on the other. Self-expression is the
fruit of the tree that conceals the serpent. The teacher is moved by
two conflicting impulses, on the one hand to encourage self-
expression and on the other to stifle it. It is out of this dilemma that
the distinction between the legitimate and the non-legitimate in
self-expression emerges. What form this distinction takes in the
case of any particular teacher is determined largely by his own
values as they have evolved through his experience in his social
milieu. What is certain, however, is that in so far as the nature of the
expressive act itself remains shrouded in mystery, the ambivalence
towards self-expression which dominates the teachers' praxis will
also persist. The teacher's ambivalence spreads very quickly to the
pupil who also comes to view self-expression with the same mixture
of suspicion and fascination. The negative ambience that results is
certainly not conducive to the pursuit of self-expression and therefore to the full use of the possibilities of the creative arts in schools.

The teacher's ambivalence towards self-expression determines not only his personal conception of legitimate and non-legitimate expression, but also the entire stance he takes with respect to both the creative process and the curriculum. This stance consists in seeking to bring the pupil's impulse into the teacher's 'context of legitimacy'. Both the impulse of the pupil and the context of legitimacy are essential to the teacher, because for self-expression to be valid in his own terms it must be determined by impulse and yet, to be acceptable, it must meet the requirements of a context of legitimacy externally imposed. Anything which falls outside this context of legitimacy is by definition a non-legitimate or socially unacceptable expression. The context of legitimacy has many facets for the teacher, among them the fact that it enables an expressive form to be placed upon some scale of value in accordance with the norms and values that are implicit in such a context. This is a point I shall take up in more detail when we come to deal with the assessment process. For the moment it is only necessary to observe that this context of legitimacy is also the basis for evaluating an expressive act as being acceptable or otherwise. The problem for the teacher, in his praxis is how to marry both the impulse that bestows validity, and the context of legitimacy that denotes acceptability, in the pupil's acts of self-expression. His stance with respect to both the creative process and the curriculum can be understood as an attempt to achieve just this.

There are two aspects to the problem of legitimacy for the teacher, although both stem from the failure of the teacher's praxis to comprehend the creative process. This failure leaves the teacher's praxis external to the pupil's creative act. He comes to define his rôle in respect of the pupil's self-expression as that of facilitating self-expression where possible and inhibiting it where necessary. This facilitative-inhibitive role is something of a tight-rope for the teacher to balance on. He is continually exposed to two sources of risk, each with its attendant anxieties. The first risk is that of facilitating self-expression which within the regulative social context is non-legitimate, and inhibiting self-expression which is legitimate within that context. To the extent that his praxis as a teacher does not comprehend the creative process and remains external to the expressive act itself, he continually runs this risk because the line between the legitimate and non-legitimate in respect of the regulative social context must be repeatedly drawn on the basis of criteria which are arbitrary, fluctuating and frequently irrelevant to self-expression. The second risk that he runs is that in attempting to increase the effectiveness of his praxis in respect of rationalising the curriculum and facilitating both a quantitative and qualitative change in the pupil's self-expression over time, his praxis begins to counter and distort the very process of self-expression that it seeks to facilitate. Again, to the extent that his praxis as a teacher does not comprehend the creative process and remains external to the expressive act he must continually run this second risk also, for the creative process is disciplined on the inside and it either resists rationalisations that are imposed far beyond it or it buckles under them. It is through imposing such external rationalisations, while maintaining a strongly facilitative orientation, that many an arts teacher seeks to convince himself that his praxis truly comprehends the creative process and is implicated in it. Careful examination of the teacher's praxis reveals that this is usually not the case. The arts teacher rarely involves himself in the process of developing or evoking the sensate disturbance within the pupil which is to be the origin of the pupil's self-expression. He provides a space and a set of instructions, and his own praxis really becomes engaged only with what emerges. In this he is rather like a gardener who pays no attention to times of planting, to the soil or what goes on underneath it, but waits till a plant emerges above the soil from somewhere and then sets about the task of getting it to grow in the direction he wants. In between times, of course, he has his hands full with weeding. If he keeps really busy he may not notice that for all his efforts there are very few flowers in his garden.

Given that the teacher confronts these two risks, that of facilitating the non-legitimate and inhibiting the legitimate, on the one hand, and that of being ineffective or negatively effective in his praxis, on the other, it is hardly surprising that his stance in respect of the curriculum can be understood as a series of stratagems for reducing the level of these risks. The risks arise, however, because the teacher's praxis remains external to the pupil's self-expression. For such a teacher the more completely he orients the curriculum and his praxis towards the pupil's self-expression and individuality, the higher is the level of both risks. To reduce the level of risk without actually comprehending the creative process and involving his praxis on the inside of the pupil's expressive act, the teacher must retreat from self-expression and individuality. The arts teacher thus brings into the curriculum a dialectical contradiction involving, on the one hand, a strong drive towards the fostering of self-expression as a central validating principle of the creative arts, and an equally strong drive in the opposite direction away from self-expression in order that the teacher can sustain an adequate level of personal security by lowering the risks to that security to acceptable levels. Some of the stratagems used by teachers to handle this contradiction will emerge in the second part of this work which deals with empirical instances of the praxis of teachers. For the moment I propose only to look briefly at some of the factors that influence the level of risk to the teacher that can be attributed to the characteristics of the medium in which the expressive act takes place. I will use the media involved in the four subjects that formed the basis of the empirical study in Part Two. These are English, drama, art, and music.

(*a*) *English*: When it comes to the use of verbal media for self-expression quite high levels of risks are involved, contrary to the claims of many English teachers. In the first place the use of words is heavily socialised, much more so than visual form. Words have such a vital function in the cognitive and interactive processes that socialising agencies are apt to subject them to the most rigorous social control when it comes to self-expression. If the pupil were truly to express himself freely in verbal media, or if he even knew how to, the context of legitimacy would be evoked at once. This is not simply a matter of the content of the self-expression offending. That may certainly be part of it. It is equally a matter of the form of the expression being non-legitimate. Verbal form conveys not only aspects of the individual's reasoning but also his whole mode of relationship to others and to the world around him. Non-legitimate modes of verbal expression often convey non-legitimate attitudes. The individual who uses them is perceived not merely as being improperly dressed but as being indecently exposed. The conditions of life for many of the youngsters in our urban schools would give rise to radically different orientations in the use of verbal media which would convey radically different social attitudes if self-expression was not so strictly inhibited both at home and at school. Words have implications that tilt at the world of action, and words are used to establish a considerable measure of social control over action. As the implications of the child's speech become clear they are evaluated as more or less legitimate. So all-pervasive and automatic is the social control of verbal behaviour that the teacher often perceives himself to be facilitating self-expression at the precise moment when he is inhibiting it most. This is an argument I shall take up in more detail later. So far as the curriculum is concerned, the pupil's modes of verbal discourse reflect his structuring of object relations, even those that include him as an object. Curricula in the humanities and the liberal arts make strong demands upon the pupil to use speech in ways that reflect a progressive improvement in his grasp of the 'facts of life'. Verbal behaviour is more easily perceived as legitimate when it articulates the world as fact that is valid independently of the existence of the speaker. The more that personal and subjective sensate experience dominates speech, the less legitimate is such speech perceived to be. Within the context of the school curriculum verbal behaviour is very much the servant of objectivity. The curriculum is very largely devoted to the development of the object centred perspective in the furtherance of rational action in the world. Subject-centred speech is often experienced as alarming because it makes claims upon the world that are independent of logical principles and rational action. These claims are often perceived as anarchical in origin to the extent that the intelligence of feeling is not comprehended by the teacher's praxis.

Nevertheless, the English teacher is strongly committed to the idea of self-expression and, as I have stated, this always involves on the part of teachers a recognition of the sensate impulse, the subjective component in expression. Equally, however, the teacher is motivated to move in the opposite direction, away from the sensate impulse towards the constraints of objective order. The resolution suggested by the verbal medium springs from its dual rôle as both a medium of impression and a medium of expression. The use of the medium can be subtly balanced so that in a single statement there is both impression and expression. One of the best examples of this is the expression of a value judgement or a personal opinion. The expression of value judgements in English lessons is highly socialised both in form and content. The teacher is able to control them not only in his determining of subject matter, of what is to be talked about, but more particularly, in his influence in determining in what ways it is appropriate to talk about the subject matter. The objective frame of reference imposed by the teacher dominates the discourse and it will only accept those value judgements on the part of the pupil that find a place within it. In other words the pupil can express himself provided that in doing so he does not attempt to undermine the rational framework within which the discourse is carried on. The sensate impulse of the pupil can find expression to the extent that it can take on any of the forms that are legitimate in the context of this rational framework. Thus in discussing characters, passions or authors in English literature, pupils are encouraged to express their own subjective views in logical discourse about them. Passion is not to be met with passion in expression but with thoughts about passion.

The possibilities for using verbal media for both impression and expression within a single form, the value judgement, provide the English teacher with his most important means of resolving the contradiction between his need to facilitate self-expression on the one hand and to inhibit on the other. This contradiction only arises, however, to the extent that the creative process and the act of self-expression are not comprehended by the teacher's praxis and remain external to it. When this is no longer the case then the teacher's praxis will embrace the self-expression of the pupil in ways that will lead to the full use of verbal media in creative reading and creative writing, and the use of English studies as the careful structuring of value judgements will decline. The value judgement will lose in importance only in the sense that it will cease to be the pivot of English studies simply because there will be no need to use its special properties to resolve a conflict that would no longer exist.

(*b*) *Drama*: Drama, which is really a composite medium, presents the teacher with somewhat different problems for resolving the contradiction of self-expression. Dramatic form is potentially more threatening than verbal form alone. For one thing it frequently subsumes the latter. It is also much closer to action in the world. In dramatic form the individual's own person is used not merely as the agent of expression (as in painting a picture or composing a piece of music) but also as the medium of expression. It is this use of the person as the medium that brings drama so close to action. In drama the pupil's person and expressive form are one, and the teacher is obliged to confront the former in the latter and vice versa. The two risks mentioned earlier are at their highest in drama. Firstly there is a greater likelihood that the teacher will facilitate expression that is illegitimate within the terms of his regulative social context, while inhibiting expression that is legitimate within that context. Also there is a greater likelihood that his praxis will distort the expressive act that it seeks to facilitate in the attempt to be effective with respect to it. Both risks are the result of the externality of self-expression to praxis and they are most powerfully in evidence where expression comes closest to action itself. Here the threat of what I have called subject-reactive behaviour is most keenly felt.

In drama there are possibilities for resolving the teacher's dilemma with respect to the expressive contradiction, as in English. Some drama is so very close to action that the teacher can make use of the logic of social constraints operating in real social situations to control dramatic improvisation. The role play is ideal here. The pupil is required to innovate and to express himself but within the constraints of a social situation and the mutual expectations of people playing other rôles within that situation. Thus the teacher can bring the regulative social context directly to bear upon the pupil's expression simply by incorporating it into the dramatic exercise that he initiates. Thus children can be encouraged to act out any number of different rôles in different social contexts from being prisoners of war to debating a compulsory house purchase order in relative safety. The teacher simply has to develop the situation in ways that ensure that the logical constraints of the situation are not lost upon the pupil who comes to perceive his task as that of establishing socially appropriate forms of behaviour. To ensure that the logic and social constraints of the situation are fully comprehended by the pupil the drama teacher will often resort to extensive discussion both before and after the improvisation. Between them the rôle play and the discussion provide the teacher with the safety net he needs. They resolve the contradiction between the teacher's need to facilitate and inhibit self-expression.

(c) *Art*: The use of visual form within the context of the art lesson does not provide the same degree of threat to the teacher as does the use of verbal and dramatic media. In part this is a consequence of the nature of the medium itself. Visual representations play an important but subordinate rôle in the everyday business of communication and interaction. They are further removed from action itself than words or gestures, both in the sense that they are not primarily used to control action as are words, nor do they make use of the individual's own person as the medium of expression as do gestures. It is in the area of content rather than form that visual representations can be perceived as threatening. Representations of the socially taboo are somewhat less threatening than enactments, but they arouse considerable anxiety nevertheless. The history of erotic art is certainly a testimony to that. However, in the art lesson the potential threat of visual representation is something which rates relatively low in the consciousness of the teacher. In addition to the nature of the medium, the creative act and the conditions under which it takes place, are more easily controlled in the art lesson. Teacher and pupil communicate with one another in relative privacy concerning individual productions. The creative process is largely confined to the individual, and his expression builds slowly permitting a great deal of interaction between him and the teacher before it is complete. Finally it is an inexpedient way to convey the socially taboo as the ratio of words to pictures on lavatory walls will testify.

The art teacher's praxis does not comprehend the creative process any more than does that of the English or drama teacher and consequently it remains external to that process. Even so the art lesson admits of a great deal more self-expression simply because the level of personal threat experienced by the teacher in respect of the pupil's sensate impulse is so low. Nevertheless, the context of legitimacy concerns not only the socially taboo but also the validity of the expressive act. To the extent that the teacher's praxis remains external to the creative process it is excluded by it. The teacher is then left continually questioning the validity of what he is doing in respect of the curriculum. This raises the risk that he will seek to impose some external rationalisation upon the pupil's self-expression in order to render his own praxis more effective, and in so doing distort the very process he is seeking to facilitate.

With the increase in this second risk the teacher may well resort to another solution. Whereas words are discursive symbols that can be used in combination both expressively and impressively, visual representations are iconic symbols that can be used both expressively and impressively. In art a subtle blend of the two is achieved in the elements that go to make up 'design education'. Here, too, there is reference to an external and objective framework in respect of which the individual's expression is legitimated, a rational context. The individual expresses himself within the imposed frame of reference and provided his expression is legitimate within that frame of reference and does not undermine it then it is admitted.

DESIGN AND
TECHNOLOGY

Design education thus enables the teacher to resolve the contradiction between the facilitating and the inhibiting of the expressive act which results from the externality of his praxis to the creative process. Design education in art is important in its own right, but if the teacher's praxis comprehended the creative process it would cease to fulfill this particular function or to hold so large an area of the stage.

(d) *Music*: Musical forms are relatively pure forms of expression in that they permit a more complete abstraction of the sensory aspects of our encounters with the world than do the other expressive media. Nevertheless, music brings with it all the associations with the world of encounters from which it grows, and it too can engender considerable anxiety in certain situations by virtue of what it expresses. One has only to think of the touchiness with which many church dignitaries react to the inclusion of musical forms that carry associations that they consider to be other than religious. However, within the context of the music lesson in school the emotional significance of different forms of music figures very indirectly as a source of threat. Indeed it is hardly able to figure at all simply because of the complete bifurcation of the creative process in music into the creative act of the composer, and the interpretive act of the instrumentalist. For the most part it is the interpretive act that dominates music in schools and not the creative act of the composer. To understand in part why this should have come about we need only to compare musical form with visual, verbal or dramatic media. While it is true that a play is also created twice, once by the author and then by the director and cast who interpret it, the play as a form is rather different from the musical composition for most people. To appreciate the play in written form one must minimally possess an understanding of the meanings of the words. Also, one must have considerable experience of the dramatic use of words in social interaction. Such experience is part and parcel of the most basic socialisation of the young. To appreciate a musical score in written form also requires minimally an understanding of the notation and a considerable experience of the use of sounds in musical expression. Such experience is not necessarily part and parcel of the basic socialisation of the young. To some extent we must all talk creatively but there is less onus upon us to use sound creatively. To the extent that such experience is not built up naturally in our basic socialisation the use of realised form comes to dominate our approach to music. The enactment of music that has already been made assures a major significance in introducing us to the meaning of music whereas the natural rôle play of childhood introduces us to drama as a creative act. So great are the demands of the instrumentality in music, however, that they dominate the consciousness of musicians. The problems of enactment, of performance, become completely separated in the formal training of musicians from those of composing music. In drama the individual's own person is used as the medium of expression, and it is a skill that does not respond easily to formal training, but in music where the individual's person is used as the agent of an expressive act in which the instrument is of such importance, the training factor assumes much more importance. Instrumental skill is no less a natural facility than dramatic skill but it responds more easily to the corrective attention of the teacher provided the initial facility is there. In part this is because the enactment in drama requires a much more sensitive and creative response on the part of each of the actors towards one another in the enactment whereas in music (of the type that dominates musical training) 'solo' performances are synchronised in the enactment in a much more mechanical way. It is the 'solo' requirements of the training in music that make the training figure so largely whereas in drama the spontaneous interactive sensitivity dominates and, as a skill, more easily excludes and eludes the teacher.

There are a variety of reasons that have led to the strongly instrumentalist bias in formal music education, and I have only touched briefly on one or two. My point in raising them has not been to explore the matter fully but simply to indicate why music differs from the other creative arts in respect of the logic of its praxis with regard to self-expression. Quite simply, to the extent that the instrumentalist's skills dominate the teaching of music, the problem of self-expression hardly arises. There are real signs that this is already changing, not only in schools but in modern music which is placing new emphasis on improvisation, instrumental interactions and the awareness of creativity and performance. To the extent that this occurs in teaching the contradiction of self-expression arises once more and demands resolution as it does in art, drama, and music.

The teacher of the creative arts is invariably an advocate of self-expression and individuality and often pursues them as ideals in the construction of his curriculum. His ambivalence with regard to self-expression springs from the fact that to the extent that his praxis does not comprehend the creative process it cannot become involved in the expressive act. It is inside the creative process that the expression grows, and involvement from the outside can often distort and inhibit the very expression that the teacher seeks to facilitate. Add to that the problem of the social taboos that surround sensate experience, and it is not difficult to see why teachers clutch at self-expression as though it were a lustrous rose in a forest of thorns.

2 Control of the medium

The expressive act consists of the projection of sensate impulse through an expressive medium, the outcome of which is a feeling-form. The very life of the expressive act is its sensate impulse and if this ceases to guide it then it is no longer an expressive act. All expressive activity, therefore, 'follows impulse'. Nevertheless the individual can look at the expressive form in terms of the way in which it is put together as object. An analysis of the structure of a piece of music or a description of the compositional logic of a painting, rules of perspective and so forth, are all instances of apprehending the expressive form as object, of assimilating it in object-knowing. This knowing of the expressive form as object has an important function even apart from keeping arts critics in business. It provides a storehouse of solutions to problems, a storehouse of facts, techniques, effects, etc. which the individual can make use of in expression *but only to the extent that his usage of them is controlled by impulse in process as it were and to the extent that such usage recalls his sensing.* In other words a rule or convention of expressive form in music or drama or whatever, can have no value in expression unless the individual is able to use it to express his sensate impulse, and he can only do this if his actual realisation of the rule is controlled by impulse. Thus, when looked at from the outside, the regularities in an artist's work may allow of description in terms of rules but when seen from the inside such regularities are purely determined and controlled by the artist's impulse. If he is being truly expressive, the rule or convention does not represent for him the constraining regularity that it does for the critic or observer. It fulfils his own impulse behaviour. It is his personal expressive act. Under the control of impulse old regularities give way to new, not in the sense that the artist seeks to transform one rule into another, but in the sense that the impulse guides behaviour from the inside in ways that can only be described from the outside in terms of rules, and variations or changes in rules.

The vast body of rules, techniques, conventions, and practices that constitute the heritage of expressive form are an immense threat to the expressive act itself. They give rise to the possibility of organising expressive forms on the outside of the self, or producing forms by application of rules. Images can be painted, sequences of dance steps enacted, music composed and performed, without being controlled or directed by feeling-impulse at all, without being self-expressive. Forms empty of feeling can arise simply by virtue of our capacity to grasp and then reproduce external regularities. Naturally artists are contemptuous of such forms for they have nothing to do with subject-knowing, indeed they are a deadening influence on the very pulse of sensate life, but art itself is never entirely free of them. There is a continuing dialectic between the impulse and the rule, between life and that which would freeze it.

We can convey this dialectic between impulse and rule in respect of the problem that the individual has in controlling the medium in which he is expressing himself. There are two possibilities. His control of the medium is either *rule-directed* or it is *reflexive*. If his control of the medium is rule-directed then his form is put together as object. The external regularities control the shaping of his behaviour, the object is master. When control of the medium is rule-directed it can never be truly self-expressive. In self-expressive behaviour the individual can make use of what are called rules but he cannot use them *as rules*. They lose that status when impulse makes behaviour its own.

In opposition to rule-directed control of the medium is what I have called 'reflexive' control of the medium. Reflexive control is fundamental to the creative process. Here it is the sensate impulse that is master. The behaviour of the individual is shaped by the inner movement of sensate impulse which is projected through the expressive medium. In order to control the development of form in the expressive act, however, the consciousness of the individual must 'oscillate' intensively between the impulse and the medium. Only in this way can the impulse (which in itself is blind) be guided by its effect in the medium. It is this oscillation which is the basis of reflexive control. It has nothing to do with organising the medium objectively. It is the to-and-fro movement whereby a feeling-impulse is brought together with its effect upon the expressive medium in the ongoing creative process, and is thereby enabled to make the continuous fine adjustments in expressive behaviour required to realise feeling in the release of the impulse.

To pursue reflexive control of the medium, the teacher's praxis must become involved inside the pupil's expressive act. Even where the pupil is making use of established conventions in musical or visual form or whatever, if he is doing so reflexively, then his sensate impulse has made them its own. They are its choice and not its prison. The problem that the teacher has in helping the pupil to control the medium in which he is expressing himself is precisely the same as the problem he has in initiating self-expression in the pupil in the first place. His praxis is simply external to the pupil's self-expression. Rule-directed control of the medium tends to dominate the praxis of arts teachers, but always with a great many misgivings and frequent retreats into relative anarchy. This fundamental dissatisfaction with rule-directed control of the medium springs from the ambivalence in arts teachers with regard to self-expression. To the extent that the arts teacher seeks to meet the demands of self-expression, rule-directed control of the medium appears as threatening that self-expression. On the other hand, to the extent that he seeks to prevent the 'illegitimate' expression or to increase the effectiveness of his praxis, he finds himself resorting more and more to rule-directed control of the medium. Often he ends up in a kind of limbo where he is able to offer the child no kind of real assistance in controlling the medium, but he can cheer him on from the sidelines, always assuming of course that there is something to cheer him on for. Some of the braver teachers who have thrown out rule-directed control in order to free the pupil's expressive act, have often been deeply frustrated by their failure to achieve this effect. They have relinquished rule-directed control but reflexive control of the medium has still eluded them. Relinquishing rule-directed control does not of itself involve their praxis inside the pupil's expressive act.

3 Use of realised form

In the expressive form the individual recalls his sensing, he knows it in feeling. So far we have concerned ourselves solely with expressive form as it is shaped by the individual's impulse, expressive form as his own creation. But what about the relationship between his sensing and expressive forms created by others, forms that are already *realised*? Works of art, paintings, symphonies, plays, poems, the treasury of forms that already exist and to which he may be exposed, how can he make use of these in subject-knowing?

The appreciation of realised form is an active process and one that does not differ in many essential characteristics from consciousness as it is implicated in the creation of expressive form. It is true that the form does not arise out of the individual's own sensate impulse, but it is also the case that the work remains unappreciated to the extent that it does not realise sensate impulse for him. In other words the sensing that the work evokes in him must reverberate with his being in ways that recall sensate impulse in addition to enlarging sensate impulse. If the disturbance wrought within him by the expressive form is too distant from sensing already present then there will be no reverberation between them and he cannot use the form to know his Being. The use of realised form therefore implies that there exists sensing within the individual that his use of the form can both recall and interact with. The appreciation of realised form is an active process because although the individual's sensate impulse does not create the form it usually guides the search for it and always the use of it. The realised form may incorporate a variety of possibilities for subject-knowing. The individual must find his way in it, explore all its possibilities, or more correctly, all the possibilities it has for him. He must actively engage the form, probe it with his sensing until echoes of that sensing return to him and he knows his Being. It is often said of great works of art that they can be appreciated on many different levels. By this it must surely be meant that a great wealth of sensate impulse can be realised through them, that their sensate possibilities are many, deep, and various. We say of them that they have universal appeal. By this it cannot be meant that each individual man responds to them in the same way as every other individual man. Rather each man may know his individual Being in the world through his use of such universal realised forms. The use of such forms is ultimately as individual as are the Beings of those who use them.

The appreciation of realised form plays a very considerable part in the teaching of the creative arts in schools, more particularly in

English studies and music and somewhat less so in the art and drama lessons. However, teachers often have the greatest difficulty in leading pupils to engage actively in realised form, to find their way in it, and to use it to realise and develop sensate impulse. The teacher often makes use of realised forms for which the pupil does not have adequate sensate experience to enable him to engage in the form. There is often a tendency on the part of the teacher to treat of the sensate possibilites of the form as though they were self-evident, or rather evident to all selves. Nothing could be further from the truth. The active probing of the form and the gradual assimilation of the sensing it evokes to sensing already present in the individual is an exercise which requires more than simple concentration. It requires some reasonable possibility that the pupil's probing of the form will yield sensing close to that which guides the probe.

Again, the teacher's problem in using realised form effectively derives from the externality of his praxis to the pupil's expressive act. To develop the use of realised form as a means of subject-knowing he needs to involve his praxis inside the pupil's expressive act. Only then can he help the pupil to express himself in his use of realised form. So long as the teacher's praxis remains external to expressive action, the selection and deployment of realised form in the curriculum is likely to be made upon the basis of criteria which are irrelevant to the pupil's expressive action. This is particularly the case in English and music lessons for example. However, not only is the selection frequently made upon the basis of criteria that are irrelevant but the actual use that is made of the realised form bears the powerful imprint of external rationalisation. 'Criticism' and 'critic talk' easily become the normal mode of registering encounters with realised form. Again there is some element of expression involved as with the expression of value judgements in the discussions and debates of English lessons, but the external frame of reference and the dictates of rationality dominate. It is not purely 'sour grapes' that motivates so many artists to speak with deep suspicion of 'criticism'. The critic is engaged in a rather different exercise, one which is largely discursive and which talks about feeling without evoking it. Some critics do of course evoke sensate experience in their work. To the extent that they do so they are using realised form in a truly expressive and creative way and what they do is not what the artist often rejects as 'criticism'. In schools, however, it is criticism of the non-creative type that usually dominates the curriculum.

Realised form is also used to provide opportunity for enactment. The so-called performing arts—music, dance, and drama, etc.—make use of realised form in this sense. As I have already argued, the performance aspect figures particularly prominently in music in schools, which it tends to dominate. It also figures to some small extent in drama lessons and dance. In most cases, however, the teacher's praxis and its relationship to the creative process ensures that the selection of material for enactment and the guidance of the process of enactment has little if anything to do with the expressive needs of the pupil or the sensate possibilities that he might realise. This is not always the case, of course. Sometimes teachers are lucky and sometimes their intuition is particularly well developed. When the latter is the case their praxis really does comprehend the creative process and is integrally deployed in the pupil's expressive act.

4 Personal development

The personal development of the pupil is really the whole *raison d'être* of arts curricula. By 'personal development' is meant the child's progressive mastery of new and more complex levels of sensate experience. Naturally his progress in controlling expressive media is part of this but it is by no means the most important part. The pupil must come to respond to sensate problems that perhaps formerly could not be evoked within him and he must use his response, his feeling-impulse, to recall his sensing and thereby resolve the sensate problem. Progress is measured in terms of the complexity of sensate problems that he can handle. The elaboration of the world of sensate experience for the pupil constitutes his personal development in the most intimate sense possible. It is the making of his feeling response in respect of the world in which he has his Being.

How are we to conceive of the increasing complexity and elaboration of sensate experience? In the first place we must distinguish between the specific content of sensate experience, the products of events in their particularity, and the structural and functional aspects of sensate experience that are universal and invariant. It is these latter aspects upon which we shall concentrate, for while it is true that the particularity of an individual's experience makes him the unique self that he is, it is also the case that specific experiences of all kinds for all individuals are subject to the same principles of functioning, the same modes of organisation, and that we can conceive of these structural-functional characteristics as invariant, in contradistinction to the specific content ordered by them which is highly variable. In other words, the experience of a 'contrast' or a 'paradox' can subsume any number of specific sensate events, for these terms are used to refer not to the content of these particular events but to the ordering of sensate experience which is universal.

My use of the term personal development is therefore restricted in this context to the development of the individual's functioning in relation to sensate experience. The point is an important one because the maturity of an individual is not based solely on his level of functioning. It is his actual functioning in respect of specific events. In short, it is life in all its particularity, in all its specific content, life as it is lived that makes for maturity. The development of more elaborate levels of functioning in respect of sensate experience makes maturity of response a possibility. It provides the means of establishing a meaningful personal relationship with the world but it does not thereby guarantee it. It is the choice of everyman that determines his Being in every moment of existence. In the commitment and process of Being, it is particularly, the specific and unique aspects of every sensate event, that is of paramount importance. Here, in existence itself, Being is led from one alone to one alone. It is the making of every instant as 'le cas pur'. The generalisation has no place in this realm. Man is able to transcend the universality of his mode of functioning, the inheritance of a nervous system, a physical body and a universe which is like those of other men. Every man's particularity is his alone, or more correctly, it is *he* alone, for true particularity is subsumed under no category and is known by no other. In existence no man can follow another. Each individual finds his own particularity. The teacher cannot enter that of the child however close he feels himself to be in understanding. His task is a different one. It is to bring about a progressive adaptation between the invariant functioning of the individual's sensate experience on the one hand, and the world in which he has his Being on the other. In so far as the world in which we live has manifested an object development which has rendered the individual inadequate in coping with the sensate problems it sets, we require to develop our sensate functioning to a level that makes possible an adequate feeling response in the world. Adequate feeling response in this sense refers solely to the universalistic and invariant modes of functioning of the individual in respect of sensate experience. His particularity is his alone in all action. He develops it in every choice that he makes, in every action that follows impulse. The curriculum therefore does not determine the child's Being, his particularity, but it plays a very large part in the development of the child's *mode* of functioning in respect of the world.

Teachers of the creative arts are usually unable to formulate objectives for personal development in respect of the child's sensate experience simply because to do so requires not only that the praxis of the teacher should comprehend the creative process, but also the process of development itself in sensate experience. At the present time, the praxis of most teachers does neither. This is not a matter of wilful neglect. It is simply that in the present stage of the development of the creative arts in schools the necessary questions and problems are only just beginning to emerge in a form that invites solution. This is not to say that the arts do not concern themselves with the problem of personal development. On the contrary in drama and English especially, all sorts of claims are made in the name of personal development. As we shall see in Part Two, however, when these are closely examined they can usually be shown to be based upon criteria of progress that are external both to sensate experience and the creative process.

5 Examinations and assessment

The assessment process has two functions. It monitors the progress of the pupil but it also monitors the effectiveness of the teaching function, of the organisation and deployment of curricula. Teachers and pupils alike are dependent upon feedback to guide their participation in the educational encounter. Nevertheless, the way in which we conceive of this feedback has important consequences for the structure of curriculum. Assessment itself implies a summation, a stock-taking operation. The individual's work is literally 'summed up'. Examination grades are the most extreme and typical forms of assessment that are used in our educational system. The individual's behaviour is transmuted into a scale of value in which all its particularity is deliberately lost. Even where examinations are not used and summary descriptions are employed instead, the basic principle is the same. The individual is given a place relative to others in a structure. It is no wonder that the examination system is at its most efficient in assessing scientific or mathematical knowledge. Assessment is the process of knowing the individual as object in relation to other individuals as objects. It is therefore at its most efficient when it differentiates between individuals as objects in relation to their knowledge of objects. It becomes something else altogether when it attempts to differentiate between individuals as objects in relation to their knowledge of their subjectivity, when by such differentiation is meant the judgement that one individual is more himself than another.

In asserting that one individual is more himself than another I am dependent upon my living contact with him and his work to make this assessment. There are no objective and universal criteria which enable me to make such an assessment. His progress in expressing himself is registered in the very particularity of his work, and my ongoing encounter with that particularity is my means of abstracting an assessment, always assuming that I wish to do so. In other words, the assessment process in respect of subject-knowing is founded on the dynamic encounter between the teacher and the particularity of the child. He is dependent upon this underlying encounter to monitor his own behaviour as indeed is the pupil to monitor his. In an ideal world perhaps this underlying dynamic encountering of one individual's particularity by that of another would be sufficient unto itself. We need not speculate on what this might mean for the future of assessment as such. We need only point out that the teacher of the creative arts only has the inner reality of the educational encounter from which to abstract an assessment. To the extent that he is obliged, through the externality of his praxis to the creative process, to seek refuge in academic assessment, in examinations, he undermines the inner reality of the encounter as the only true basis of assessment in subject-knowing and surrenders his activity and his curriculum to the dictatorship of an irrelevant externality. The academic examination can so easily be a betrayal of subject-knowing.

Throughout this chapter I have sought to argue that the logic of the teacher's praxis in the creative arts is built upon the need to resolve contradictions that arise as a result of the failure of his praxis to comprehend the creative process and to involve itself intrinsically with the pupil's expressive act. Because the teacher's praxis remains largely external to the pupil's expressive act the teacher is obliged to relate to that expressive act very much in terms of facilitating or inhibiting it from beyond. He needs to facilitate it, for self-expression is accepted by the arts teacher as a vital part of the function of the creative arts. He also needs to inhibit it, however. To the extent that the teacher does not recognise the epistemological distinction between subject-reactive and subject-reflexive behaviour made in Chapter 1, the problem of drawing the line between legitimate and non-legitimate self-expression is much more difficult. The problem is made worse by the externality of his praxis to the creative process because this leaves him less in control of the development of the expressive act. The teacher thus pulls in two directions, both facilitating and inhibiting self-expression but not necessarily developing it. The more he facilitates self-expression, the less in control he appears to be and the more risk he runs of facilitating what within his own terms is illegitimate. The more he inhibits self-expression, the more in control he appears to be, but he runs a much greater risk of inhibiting self-expression that in his own terms is legitimate, and also of distorting even that expression which he has facilitated. These pressures are expressed differently by different teachers operating in different situations or with different media. I have made no attempt to deal with individual variations and I make no claim that arts teachers either agree or are all alike in their teaching methods. What I have sought to do is to reveal what I believe to be the logical core of the praxis of arts teachers. For such a logical case to be a valid account of praxis, teachers must be able to make sense of their particular actions and situations in respect of it. A logic of praxis can only be validated in praxis. Contrary to what many cynics believe, men do not lightly take up rationalisations of what they do, which have serious implications for future action, purely on the basis of suggestion. The more susceptible is the individual's consciousness to accepting a senseless account of himself, the less is his practice able to make sense of it, and the account is therefore invalidated in praxis since praxis comprehends both consciousness and practice. The point is made in case the reader should jump to the conclusion that a different kind of claim for validity is being made, one that is external to the praxis of the teacher. The validity referred to here has nothing to do with what most laymen and too many sociologists regard as scientific validity, namely the making of statements that are valid in some sense that is external to their use in action as though praxis could be comprehended from without.

So much for the logic of praxis. In Part Two we shall move very much closer to empirical instances of praxis and, so far as is possible, illustrate and develop the argument through the consciousness of teachers themselves and also through the responses of pupils. Finally, in Part Three, I shall seek to build on the framework and critique by drawing some implications for arts teaching with respect to the problem of involving praxis inside the pupil's expressive act.

The Research

The 'Arts and the Adolescent' project carried out an extensive programme of research into the teaching of the creative arts in secondary schools. One important part of that programme involved a large pilot study of some thirty-six schools in London, Bristol, Cambridge, and the South West of England. From these, six schools were selected for intensive study. The research team spent a minimum of two weeks in each school observing lessons in English, art, music, and drama. All members of staff who taught these subjects were interviewed together with some 10% of the pupils of the school. All of the staff and the pupils were invited to complete questionnaires, and a number of other research instruments were deployed to obtain additional data. The purpose of all this was simply to enable us to get as close as possible to the many facets of the arts educational encounter as it takes place in schools. By 'educational encounter' I mean the interaction between the consciousness of a teacher and the consciousness of a pupil as mediated by the curriculum.

The research programme was explicitly designed to probe the praxis of teachers in a relatively intensive way rather than to obtain empirical data for generalisation on other educational systems. Nor did the design take place in a vacuum. It was guided by my theoretical framework concerning the function of the creative arts in the organisation of sensate experience. The analysis that follows is the result of applying that theoretical framework to the praxis of teachers as revealed by the research. The theoretical framework outlined in the first chapter not only influenced the design of the research programme, therefore, it also influenced the analysis of the results of that research programme. The theoretical framework is thus used as a mirror in which the praxis of teachers is reflected.

In the chapters that follow extensive use is made of the interviews with arts teachers. These were the most important source of data concerning the consciousness of the teachers while the observations of lessons provided a more independent guide to practice. Finally, the chapter on the pupil's responses is based largely on the results of a questionnaire administered to all pupils. A large part of the rest of the data was available to me in making the analysis and it certainly influenced the interpretation (particularly the pupil interviews), but these data have not been used to illustrate the argument. Quite simply I have used the teacher interview, observation and pupil questionnaire data to work the argument through the consciousness and practice of teachers and the stated choices and preferences of pupils.

The discussion of each of the creative arts is framed in terms of the five major areas outlined earlier. The first concerns the extent to which the arts curriculum in question fosters or encourages individualism and self-expression. The second area concerns the extent to which the design of the curriculum makes demands upon the pupil to control the medium which he is using to convey his idea. Most teachers agree that such control is necessary but the curricula for the different arts subjects reveal rather differing tendencies with respect to it, as I have argued already. The third area concerns what I have called the 'use of realised form'. Works of art, literature, music, and drama play an important part in developing appreciation but, in the case of drama and music at least, they are important from the point of view of performance as well. Teachers expose pupils to realised form, to works of art or literature, etc., in ways that have important consequences, sometimes negative, for the pupil's creative response. The fourth area concerns the personal development of the pupil and the extent to which the curriculum is organised with clear objectives in terms of the pupil's personal development with respect to the organisation of sensate experience. Again the various arts curricula differ considerably in their tendencies with respect to it. Finally, the fifth area concerns the troublesome problem of assessment. Nowhere is the problem of assessment and of examinations a more controversial subject than in the design of the arts curricula. Arts teachers frequently approach the idea of examinations with a mixture of hostility and fascination. Nevertheless the different arts curricula reveal quite distinctive tendencies with respect to the problem of assessment.

The Research

In addition to developing these five major categories, brief comments will also be made upon such things as curriculum content and structure, the mode of encounter and the structure of communication networks.

The Teachers

3   English

1   Self-expression and individuality

Almost without exception English teachers (among those to whom we talked to) endorse individualism and self-expression in their ideals of what the subject is for.

> 'I think they really need—especially the kids I deal with in this school—to express themselves, to be heard, to be listened to and, as I say, just to express themselves on the whole gamut of things in different ways, in conversation, in acting, in drama, poetry, painting or whatever. I just feel that the other subjects inhibit this kind of self-expression . . .'

This was a commonly expressed view appearing again and again in the interviews that we had with English teachers. Often self-expression was explicitly tied to 'communication', and this too was a recurring theme as one would expect.

> 'I use the lessons as a space in which people can think and review situations and be themselves and discuss whatever they want to discuss and where they can write with a view to using writing as the crystallisation of thought—where they can explore writing as a way of communicating with people, and talking as an especially valid way of communicating with people. The whole thing is the communications area in an English lesson.'

Despite the very real concern of English teachers with individualism and self-expression, the design of curricula in English reveals much less scope for it than this concern would indicate. Indeed there appeared to be a manifest tendency, in many of the English lessons that we observed, to suppress as much (if not more) as to facilitate the self-expression of the pupil. This contradiction stems in part from the rather restricted sense in which many teachers of English use the term self-expression.

As the adolescent develops he becomes increasingly capable of appreciating other viewpoints than his own, of grasping the other person's perspective, of constructing both sides of an argument, of being rational and conscious of the feelings of others. As far as the curriculum is concerned this opens up vast new possibilities for his activities in sciences and humanities and the arts. In English this challenge is usually met by opening up to the pupil the world of complex human situations, through literature, discussion of various problems, creative writing, etc.

In this process the teacher most strongly rewards evidence of objectivity on the part of the pupils, their capacity to grasp other perspectives and to be realistic in their appraisal of human situations including their own. It is this burgeoning objectivity in the pupil that delights so many English teachers, and not without reason, for it is certainly one of the great achievements of adolescent development. There are other aspects to adolescent development however, which are all too easily ignored or passed over. Adolescence is a period of stirring emotionalism, of deep shifts of affect, the discovery of passion and the embrace of commitment, of undying love of absolutes and total involvement. Does the English teacher reward expression of these? In the author's experience this is rarely the case. All of these states of consciousness appear in the curriculum particularly in connection with literature but the pupil is rewarded most strongly for his capacity to be objective towards them. As long as he can be aware of their existence with the relative detachment of an analyst and can handle such feelings as 'objects' for arrangement and comment, he receives the approval of his teacher. To be passionate himself in his expressive form results in approval only from a minority of teachers of English, and by the rest it is met with anything from bemused tolerance to positive discomfort.

Teachers believe of course that they are already providing opportunities for (sensate) self-expression in discussions about people's feelings and literature dealing with the human passions. In this they fail to realise that objective appraisal of feeling is the expression of an opinion or a point of view but it is not the direct expression of feeling. The expression of feeling does not thrive on objectivity. It thrives on a controlled subjectivity and if the consequence of discovering the subjective feeling states of others is the sacrifice of one's own subjectivity then the step has truly been a retrograde one and from the point of view of self as well as of self-expression it might be argued that the pupil is better off with the naïve egocentrism of childhood. That at least is a more dignified estate than the one to which adolescents in our schools are so often called, encouraging as it does a mixture of watery rationalism and soapy sympathy that washes the soul clean of all traces of passion.

Another and more compelling reason for the relative lack of expression of direct feeling encouraged by English teachers stems from a genuine lack of confidence on the part of most teachers when it comes to controlling or dealing with the emotional expressions of others. In some ways this is deeply rooted in our cultural heritage. We somehow feel safer when public discourse or expression is relatively dispassionate and we are easily suspicious of and alarmed by expressive 'outbursts' that call forth responses in us which are themselves laden with feeling tone. In our schools as well as in our national culture generally there is a tendency to respect deeply the claims of emotional response but to treat those claims as essentially private, to be indulged in institutionalised settings such as the art gallery or the concert hall or in the personal intimacy of the space between one's nose and the book in which it is buried. Not even the school is permitted to encroach very far upon this preserve of private feeling response. Since feeling is very little expressed in our direct contact with one another as a people it is hardly surprising that it is sometimes looked upon as dangerous, disruptive, even perverse and irresponsible when its presence is deliberately elicited by a teacher. That teachers are both aware of pressures to elicit this type of response in the pupils and are at the same time fearful or hostile to the idea is a fact which revealed itself in a number of the interviews. Often this fear of the power of emotion in the teaching situation stemmed from the teacher's sense of responsibility concerning the vulnerability of the pupil whose personal trust might result in his exposing himself in a situation which was unsuitable to respond in 'purity of heart', as it were, to such unmasking. The teacher perceives the situation in which such feeling might be released as essentially hostile and destructive of the individual, his privacy, and his independence of the will of others. This view is very well expressed in the following extract from one of our interviews with a drama teacher.

'I feel in working with the emotional development of the child you're on really dangerous ground because here you're working with the non-rational aspect of the child. You're getting at the child underneath his normal natural defences which he uses in the general run of the school in English, Chemistry or whatever. He's forced to commit himself personally, wholly to reveal himself. When you're working on their emotional playing, emotive colours, *I feel that it is dangerous because these techniques which you use in Educational Drama are used by the Harvard Business School, they've been used by Hitler; they were used by various devious people.* It's not the method but why and how it is used that is important . . . techniques can be open to abuse by any teacher.'

This particular teacher was concerned about the possibility of exploitation involved in emotional release, of the threat of deliberate manipulation. Many other teachers however were concerned about their lack of competence to deal with the emotional responses of other people. The teachers seemed to equate direct expression of feeling rather grossly with emotional excess or emotional crisis. For many of them emotional responses had some kind of medical significance. They were something requiring the attention of a doctor rather than a teacher. As one English teacher put it:

'If they feel that the world is against them I think that it's important that they should be able to write it down. Everybody feels it from time to time. *There is a danger, however, in becoming a sort of psychiatrist figure—which I think is very dangerous because you don't know everything about the child you should know if you're going to do anything medical*—and that you create problems by making the children look too far within themselves—there is a danger in getting anyone to express themselves, because once a person has exposed themselves they are immediately vulnerable and if you don't respond with discretion and compassion you're using them.'

Closer investigation reveals therefore that in many cases the lack of opportunity provided by English teachers for direct feeling expression springs from a genuine concern that they experience for the welfare of the pupil and a healthy suspicion of their own motives and competence in respect of sensate response in the pupil. Certainly given the context of school situations this concern is neither misplaced nor ill-founded. It reveals, however, a somewhat negative appraisal of the school as an environment which can engage the pupil on any other than a superficial level. I believe that the future of education lies very much with the demands for a deeper level of engagement between pupil and curriculum. This cannot be achieved, however, until fears like those expressed above have been largely overcome and those fears cannot be overcome until the normal feeling life of the individual has been delivered from the darker shades of Freud and Orwell.

Teachers themselves are sometimes aware of this problem. When English teachers were probed about their concept of self-expression and their own curricula in respect of it, some of them revealed a keen awareness of the difference between the way in which they elicit thoughts about feelings indirectly and the true direct expression of feeling. As another of our English teachers put it:

> 'Thinking is what happens after you're seeing and feeling and you're beginning to rationalise your immediate experiences. It's also a thing that makes the other experiences (seeing and feeling) more difficult because once you're thinking about seeing, or thinking about feeling, you're then doing it in a different way. *So in fact we're sabotaging their personal responses up to a point which is a very dangerous thing to do—we're working in a dangerous area . . . I recognise it's very dangerous.*'

It is very difficult in looking from an overall oberver's standpoint to be able to estimate precisely how much of the English curriculum is devoted to something like self-expression. In English the opportunity for the pupils to express themselves in creative writing of some kind is often given over to homework. In the English lessons that we actually observed self-expression in general played a very small part and the direct feeling expression discussed above was minimal, to say the least. In effect some 70% of the lessons were strongly 'academic' in their structure, concerned either with English language or more usually with working from the text of a play or book or poem in a strongly teacher-directed way. Much of this work was tied directly to an examination syllabus. Some 20% of the lessons observed involved a considerable measure of discussion (usually text-led) with pupils contributing. The pupils often appeared to enjoy the opportunity for discussion but there was little evidence of the type of involvement that would encourage development of a richer or more subtle feeling response to life. Only about 8% of the lessons observed were devoted to any kind of creative writing exercise.

With regard to the area of self-expression and individuality there appears to be a manifest tendency in English curricula to encourage these only in the context of the pupil's developing capacity to formulate his own feelings and the feelings of others with whom he comes into contact, in an objective framework that defuses them as it were. There is no evidence that the English teacher is particularly keen to handle the 'live' wire.

2 Control of the medium

Teachers of English are under some pressure at the present time concerning this problem of control of the medium. The days are gone when the English lesson was completely dominated by Latin grammar and adverbial clauses of moment. In fact in the lessons that we actually observed there were surprisingly few devoted exclusively to English language. Those that were, frequently hinged upon the appreciation of some piece of writing. Nevertheless this revolution in English teaching is not proceeding without stresses and doubts being experienced by English teachers. For one thing it has altered the relationship of the English department to others in the school. English has traditionally been looked upon by teachers in the humanities and to a lesser extent in the sciences, as a tool subject which enhances the ability of pupils to write good history or geography essays. The consequence of the increasing tolerance on the part of English teachers towards grammatical errors and stylistic clumsiness has resulted in something of a staff-room backlash from other teachers who feel that English departments may be failing them as they slide inexorably down the slippery slope to Art. The friction is expressed very well by one of the English teachers we interviewed.

'We've been accused of not teaching them enough grammar. Foreign linguists were very keen that we should do more. We claimed that we weren't teaching them to use grammar— we were teaching them to use language and we didn't care how they managed to do this. I think people outside the English department are very disbelieving about the virtues of the imagination. They claim that they [the pupils] have got plenty of imagination. What you need to do is to make them accurate.'

Nevertheless this definite move away from traditional grammar teaching is embraced by different English teachers for what are frequently widely diverging reasons. In some cases it reflects merely a recognition of the unsuitability of teaching grammar in isolation and the possibility of replacing it with a system based on responses to 'set pieces'. The pupil's work is then 'shaped' by continual assessment (and actual grading) by the teacher. The 70% of the lessons that we observed which were given over to 'academic' English concealed (and revealed) a great deal of this. This is no less a rule-directed approach to the control of the medium in which the pupil is working than is the more explicit rule direction of formal grammar teaching. Some teachers, however, perceive rule-directed control of the medium of either type as inhibiting self-expression and personal development. When they see their colleagues as having betrayed the revolution by replacing one type of rule direction with another they express profound frustration over the fact.

'I try, whenever I feel strong enough to explain what I feel about it to other English teachers—when they'll let me get a word in edgeways in between their discussions of set books and things— I think they really think I am mad sometimes—I know I'm not mad but . . . I can't seem to get it across that—what—you must care about every individual piece of writing. You mustn't standardise and scale all the time, and say this is worth six out of ten and that's eight out of ten . . . If it's improvement that you are after then the way to get this is to produce confidence, because everybody can verbalise and everybody can write eventually—it's a question of confidence.'

Control of the medium, however, involves a great deal more than the ability to speak grammatically or to respond à la mode to set pieces of literature. It does involve also a certain capacity to select and organise words in a way that truly builds one's idea. This is discovered by practice but it is enhanced not only by the teacher providing opportunity for practice but also by the teacher taking an active rôle in encouraging and assisting the pupil to control the medium reflexively in the actual process of building his idea. The teacher quoted above was among the very few teachers of English that we observed who was able to do this effectively. In her lessons she reveals a very deep concern for control of the medium but it is not concern for formal techniques or grammatical niceties. As I watched her teach I formed an entirely personal impression of the motive behind it which I would express as follows: 'Your feeling, your impulse, is important. It is a worthwhile and precious thing. It will live and take form if you can shape it in words—if you can work it through the medium and communicate it—not half of it or bits of it all mixed up with other things but the whole of it, your impulse, your feeling. It isn't easy. Words are powerful things. They can deceive you or they can take you by surprise. They can hide you or they can reveal you. Your feeling can grow through the medium of words but your feeling must control them. If your feeling moves and grows in dance or alarm or sorrow then you must build your statements to move in the same way, in dance, in alarm, in sorrow.' Whether or not this teacher would have agreed with my personal impression of her attitude is another matter. It conveys my own feeling as I watched her teach.

Despite the growing concern with self-expression and creative writing it cannot yet be said that teachers of English have forsaken their traditional formalism. The teaching of traditional grammar has largely given way to oral and written exercises centred on set pieces or texts and it is assessed and controlled in ways that realise many of the aims of the most traditional grammarians. Those teachers whose *actual practice* encourages the type of control of the medium described above are few and far between. They are growing in number, however, and the future of English teaching will be much influenced by them.

3 Use of realised form

As one might expect, teachers of English make a great deal of use of realised form, of works of literature in their teaching. The spirit of English teaching at the present time is very much in the grip of a movement to introduce the child to literature in ways that take advantage of his personal development and truly connect with his consciousness. Teachers are becoming increasingly aware of the exciting possibilities for enriching the mental life of the child by introducing him to literature which at a given stage fulfils the need of his personal development rather than the needs of academic bodies.

Nevertheless, despite these entirely hopeful signs, the movement is meeting with some difficulties. In the first place teachers have not been so quick to perceive the function of self-expression in personal development nor to recognise that their concept of personal development is in need of fundamental revision. Appreciation needs not only to be relevant to the mental life of the child but it needs also to be integrated with his expressive activity. Creative reading should not be divorced from creative writing and creative speaking. The B.B.C. has certainly pioneered this notion in many of its programmes and no doubt English teachers are working this way in many schools. In the six schools that we studied, however, the very small amount of time devoted to creative writing (8%) is an indication at least that this kind of integration between reading, writing, and speaking is not really taking place on a large scale.

On the other hand the selection of pieces of literature that were relevant to the pupil's mental life was in evidence and one felt that with the younger pupils teachers were keying in to the consciousness of the child much more than had formerly been the case. The fact is, however, that it was only for the younger pupils that this was taking place. Around about the fourth and fifth years there is a distinct change as the examination-led syllabuses take over. Suddenly the pupils are introduced to works that are not purposely keyed in to their needs from the point of view of development or related to their own creative expression.

With these older children their relationship to realised form is established on an entirely different basis. They may in fact respond enthusiastically to some works but if they do so it is due rather to the teacher's luck than to his judgement which was not the case with the younger pupils. The lack of integration within a coherent developmental framework and the break with creative writing can render the contact between the pupil's consciousness and the world of literature a fragmentary and unsatisfactory affair. Too often what passes for creative response to works of literature is merely stylised analysis, predictable, and elaborated 'critic talk' embodying those canned nuances that announce only the worldliness of the writer or speaker involved. English teachers are often responsible for reinforcing verbal behaviour of this kind. Such verbal behaviour is not simply a sign of the objectivity referred to earlier. It is a passport to success in examinations. Critic talk is exam talk so far as the English teacher is concerned and, since critics must have something to talk about, works of literature are delivered as grist for their mills. Some teachers recognise the distinction between the imaginative and the critically analytical in the pupil's responses even though they usually deny that the great emphasis given to the one is an impediment to the development of the other. One teacher put it to us this way:

'Well, the imaginative life does continue as they grow older. It assumes a different form as you go up the school—*the nature of examinations means more emphasis upon analysing other people's stuff.* But in essence the very best work doesn't make a distinction between expressive imagination and analytical comment on other people's work. I can think of a very interesting boy we had last year who did "A" levels at the age of fourteen I think—a very brilliant artist and he got grade A; and it was very fascinating teaching him in the sixth. I was teaching him "Romantics". We did Wordsworth and Constable and Blake. *His response to these people was essentially an imaginative one. He could analyse and so on but it was essentially an imaginative response.* It was fascinating to set him on the track of things which he would follow up—for example—the relationship of Constable to Wordsworth. I was sitting reading a few of Constable's letters—he was obviously interested in the paintings. He went to the Victoria and Albert and saw an exhibition of Romantic Art and his sort of jumping the gap between the two was an imaginative step rather than an analytical one. *So even later in school life when most of the tasks you are set to do are analytical ones, still the same quality of imagination survives.*'

I am afraid I do not share this teacher's optimistic conclusion. It is significant that in an interview that pressed very hard on this point there were no revelations of consistent curriculum programmes for eliciting and developing imaginative self-expression nor were there instances of a general imaginative level of response on the part of older pupils. Instead there was this example of a brilliant pupil who fascinated those who taught him but whose imaginative development was strong enough to proceed under its own steam. Many a university student will confess that he lost his ability to respond imaginatively to literature in a feeling way in direct proportion to the intense cultivation of his critical analytical faculties in the sixth form to the exclusion of creative expression.

Analysis and criticism does have an important part to play in English studies but it is in no way a substitute for, nor is it synonymous with, creative appreciation. The latter requires that realised form be closely related to the pupil's creative expression and that he express his feeling response in a direct and personal way. It requires that he make an 'artistic' response using the 'artistic' work of others. There are teachers who do work in this way but they are too few on the ground. The spirit of some of the B.B.C. programmes on creative reading and writing has not penetrated very far into the academic citadel, and teachers of English have yet to work for Art in creative writing and creative appreciation. So far the majority appear not to have relinquished the excessive emphasis upon critic talk in the pupil's written work if not in his oral pronouncements. Furthermore, the entirely dubious and patronising assumption that works of literature have civilising influences *per se* is still more prevalent in our schools than those busy riding out the new wave would care to admit. It is true engagement that produces personal development not the cold detachment of what some people are pleased to call 'finer feelings'. Engagement in this sense is of life; it is to life and it is for life.

4 Personal development

English teachers appear to be very aware of the stages of development through which the adolescent passes. Their observations are on the whole mutually consistent with one another and they confirm very strongly the views of adolescent development held by psychologists. It would appear to follow that if teachers of English are so aware of developmental changes in adolescence that their curricula would be organised to exploit developmental possibilities to the full, leading the pupil progressively from more 'primitive' to more complex and 'elaborate' modes of response. Sometimes this may be achieved. Certainly most English teachers to whom we have spoken endorse it as an aim. However, it is not as simple or as straightforward as that. When it comes to the organisation of the curriculum it is more often the concept of 'academic' development rather than personal development which guides the teacher's structuring of material. The organisation of the curriculum so often reflects the examination-led syllabus that many teachers are unable to dissociate the idea of personal development from academic success. Often they are vaguely aware of something of a conflict between the goals of self-expression and those of academic attainment but in the end many teachers of English treat the two as though they could be reconciled within the unfolding academic schema.

Even when teachers have broken away to a considerable extent from the acceptance of 'academic' development of the pupil as a fundamental objective, they do not necessarily go on to establish a perspective based upon personal development. Often they work on a spontaneous basis abdicating or claiming to abdicate responsibility for development as such. The teacher of whose lesson I spoke earlier put it this way:

'I'm not sure whether English in fact assists in the development of the child or whether it provides food at all by which to develop. I think it's a very useful process for recording or considering your own development. I don't know whether I have a function in assisting development—whether I'd want to—sounds dreadful, doesn't it?'

It has to be pointed out however that this teacher only teaches older pupils and she does so by choice.

'I choose fourteen- or fifteen-year olds. I choose older people rather than younger ones because that is the stage it seems to me when things get really interesting emotionally.'

Sometimes the teacher shows an acute awareness of the need to organise the curriculum to make the most of the developmental possibilities of the pupil. After giving a relatively clear account of the development of the pupil during the secondary school period, one teacher concluded with a statement of his objectives as follows:

'Well, I have to choose material for the lessons according to my knowledge of the classes I'm going to meet. I have to ask myself what sort of material is going first of all to raise the questions that they ought to be asking, to answer the questions that they are asking—what sort of material is going to extend their sensibility, is going to broaden their experience.'

Nevertheless, this statement of a view sincerely held is misleading if taken at face value. The organisation of this teacher's lessons

(those that were observed) was very strongly 'academic' in orientation involving a considerable degree of teacher direction with little opportunity for innovation or self-expression on the part of the pupils. This contradiction is not unusual. The consciousness of teachers, like that of the rest of us, frequently runs somewhat ahead of what we can practise.

When the teacher attempts to move outside the developmental framework provided by the examination syllabus he has considerable difficulty in formulating developmental objectives clearly. The concept of emotional development and maturity is something which becomes very important to the teacher thoughtfully trying to formulate some goal in self-expression. Nevertheless he can only convey what he means in the most general sense. The emotional development of the pupil as yet lacks its Piaget but that does not prevent teachers making an intuitive reach for what they perceive to be the objectives of personal as opposed to academic development served by the teaching of English. A not unrepresentative view might be summed up in the words of one teacher talking about what he regarded as maturity in the individual:

'I can put into words or at any rate translate into thought, even if the thought doesn't exactly get expressed in words. I can give some expressive form other than the blush or the shudder of the content, of the movement of emotion within me. So I would say that emotional maturity was a capacity to recognise and accept one's own feelings, to recognise and accept that somehow, possibly stronger, possibly weaker feelings will arise in other people and that it's part of my business as a human being living in a society to be able to—not to be boulversé by other people's emotional outbursts . . . but to accept these as part of the human condition and to be sympathetic as well as empathic . . .'

However, on the basis of what has been observed, we would have to conclude that the actual design of curricula in English as yet reveals little evidence of a clear concept of personal development beyond that implied in the structuring of the academic demands made upon the pupil. The reader is warned, however, as he was at the outset, that empirical generalisations apply only to the schools we researched. I myself believe that these conclusions do have a much wider relevance but no statistical claims are made in respect of that.

5 Examinations and assessment

The whole notion of assessment and examination is a controversial one throughout the educational system at all levels but nowhere is the controversy more keenly felt than in connection with the arts curricula. In general the more the teacher's sights are trained towards the goals of self-expression and personal development the greater the conflict he experiences with the formal framework of 'academic' examinations. As we have seen many English teachers design their curricula to serve academic goals. I have also argued that their consciousness often runs ahead of current practice. English teachers are not as easy in their minds with the trappings of the formal examination as their strongly academic orientation would indicate. Perhaps the fairest summing up would be to say that they hold mixed and frequently contradictory views concerning them. It is a subject, however, that is inviting an increasing degree of polarisation of viewpoint. The head of an English department, himself intimately involved with examinations and the preparation of the pupils for them, had this to say:

'I think usually that they [examinations] are totally irrelevant to the essence of English—that they are designed for examiners rather than pupils—that the English literature exams as a rule *are just crimes against adolescents and against teaching.* I think the "A" level is absolutely shocking.'

When asked whether he was against examinations in principle this teacher revealed something of the dilemma that most teachers are in concerning them.

'I think Yes! would be my first answer, but it isn't an honest answer, and therefore I can't give it, because to be against examinations is to imply that I have something definite to put in their place. I would like to change them very much. *I would like the C.S.E. principle to be adopted that if you trust somebody to teach a child, you can also trust him to examine the child.* This means that the examination never works through catching people out, that it can be relevant to the work done—*that the people who are doing the work can decide what is worth doing and then examine it in the way it ought to be examined. I would much prefer C.S.E. in its approach —it has status problems obviously.*'

Most of the teachers of English whom we interviewed seem to be in favour of some sort of assessment. They would, in many cases, like to see the criteria for assessment determined much more closely by their own objectives in teaching. For this reason there is widespread endorsement among arts teachers generally for the type of of changes initiated by the advent of the C.S.E. The reason for a considerable degree of ambivalence on the part of English teachers with regard to the whole problem of assessment derives from a number of factors of the most critical kind, the importance of which can hardly be overestimated. It is assessment by examination that binds schools to the locus of authority beyond the school with 'hoops of steel'.

To assess someone is to determine his relative value. To do so with a formal declaration such as that embodied in a certificate is to hand that person a negotiable cheque, one that can be cashed at face value only at the National Society's Bank of Opportunities. It is to say to that person, 'No matter what you think you're worth, no matter how deeply you feel or how gentle are your thoughts, you are worth no more and no less than the paper you are written on.' Teachers have themselves worked for and earned these negotiable cheques and in many cases they simply accept them as facts of life. The more the teacher is oriented towards personal development and expression, however, the more difficult it is to swallow such a fact. The teacher who seeks to develop in the pupil an intelligence of feeling works with coin that is not negotiable and the value of which is beyond estimate. For such a teacher to say to a pupil, Your value has been fixed at four "O" levels', betokens something of an act of desecration. It would almost be more honourable to say as we do to so many who receive no negotiable cheques, 'In our wisdom we have found you to be worth nothing at all.'

In so far as arts teaching is moving into the area of developing an intelligence of feeling, it is also engendering in those most affected by it a complete revulsion against the traditional academic examination. This very revulsion, however, poses a considerable personal threat to the teacher concerned from two main quarters. In the first place the teacher must cope with the fact that his own professional status is intimately tied up with the status accruing to examinations. This pressure works upon him in an invidious way. In the first place he occupies his position because he has himself risen from the ranks of such a system. How much responsibility he will be given or how much access he has to intelligent youngsters will be determined by how disciplined and well trained a 'show jumper' he proved to be when rising through the ranks. If he should 'lapse' after gaining access to his profession in this way he will soon discover that promotion prospects and professional advancement are intimately tied to the standards of academic performance in examinations for which he is responsible. It is not a matter of simply counting the grades a teacher gets on behalf of his pupils in public examinations. It is far more subtle than that. If staff-room nostrils twitch with the faint odour of heresy, they positively flare at the recognition of treason. When the coin of the realm has been debased the teacher is not for burning. Cooling out is the fate that usually awaits him; to be surrounded by the great wall of indifference and to face its simple challenge: 'Give all for what you believe, or give in like the rest of us!'

Even if a teacher survives all the professional dangers of taking a stand there is a far greater pressure upon him ensuing from the felt needs of pupils and parents alike. The social race for negotiable cheques is on with a vengeance. Few pupils are going to thank a teacher who leaves them disadvantaged in this race and parents will mount considerable pressures on head teachers of schools that harbour such recalcitrant teachers. One head of an English department who expressed her revulsion against the system of traditional academic examinations concluded by saying:

'. . . But at the moment I can't take on the whole world. We have obligations to be democratic and you must be democratic. You must say to a parent—Look, its all right. At the end of this— what appears to be a very undisciplined system—your daughter who's got tremendous ability will emerge with a C.S.E Mode 1. If the kids need these at present for getting into further education or getting the jobs which they should have then it is an obligation.'

The issue of assessment is an even more critical one in education than teachers themselves are inclined to realise. The future of the teaching profession as a whole is intimately bound up with this issue and the status of teachers will grow in direct proportion to the extent to which their control over the criteria and management of the assessment process grows. This cannot happen, however, until consciousness of curriculum objectives reaches a level of refinement and elaboration in respect of the personal development of the pupil which truly distinguishes it from the traditional objectives. This has certainly not happened yet, and the English curricula are no exception. On the whole the English teachers we interviewed gave an impression of uncertainty in the face of what to them seem like insurmountable obstacles both public and professional.

In devising ways of assessing people we usually think that we are providing information about them. Very often we are doing the opposite. We are losing what information we have about them by transmuting it all into an examination grade. If a grade is to be a comprehensive summary embracing the entire quality of a person's mode of engagement with the world then it will have to be arrived at by quite different forms of assessment from those used to establish examination grades. In a world where such new forms of assessment were practised one wonders whether the need for grades or abrupt summaries of people would not by then have largely disappeared.

Curriculum structure

I have of course touched upon this in relation to the categories developed above. There it was pointed out that the English curriculum was developmentally organised in ways largely determined by examination-led syllabuses. To that extent it is not the personal development of the pupil that controls the structure of the syllabus but the criteria of cultural sophistication used by those who devise examinations. Their sights are trained upwards and outwards. The pupil does not pay the piper but he does dance to the tune.

So far as the internal structure of the lesson is concerned the English teachers that we observed usually provided a consistent structure with a definite theme of some kind. In only a few cases could one describe the internal structure of the lesson as disordered or non-existent.

Curriculum content

As in the case of structure, the content of the English curriculum is frequently determined by the set work of the syllabus. Although English teachers organise a great deal on the basis of set pieces of work, it is also true that they frequently innovate a great deal employing ingenuity and imagination in an endeavour to present content in ways that enable the pupil to identify more easily with the problems raised in texts. It is in this area of making the sauce to serve with the dish that teachers of English allow themselves some discretionary control. Some make no use of it. Many make some use of it, while a few make so much use of it that they are brought to the borders of real creative work.

Mode of encounter

As has been stated some 70% of the lessons that we observed in English were what could be described as relatively formal 'academic' lessons. The mode of encounter was that of working from a prepared text of some kind or being formally taught some aspect of English language. The 20% of lessons dominated by discussion were by no means free of prepared texts as the focus and origin of the lesson. Indeed most of the discussions observed were worked around some text or other. In the 8% of lessons devoted to creative writing there was some evidence of a breakaway from the traditional formula. However this was really an extension of primary school work in the secondary school. It has to be noted that of the six lessons devoted to creative writing, four were used with first- and second-year classes. The two remaining lessons were conducted by one teacher with a fourth-year group. It must be remembered of course that we are talking only about some seventy English lessons selected for observation in six different schools at different times during the first two terms. A much larger sample might have revealed a more balanced picture but there will be few English teachers who would claim that the *lesson time* given to the exploration of the pupil's creative writing will add up to anything but a very small percentage indeed when it comes to classes for older pupils.

Communication networks

The common form of the English lesson involves the teacher in the traditional use of a single channel of communication between him and the class. He speaks to the class as a whole. They speak to him as individuals. Comments made by pupils in response to one another are channelled through the 'chair', so to speak. This pattern is not always strictly adhered to. It is often varied and sometimes it is scrapped altogether but very rarely. With one or two notable exceptions, the teachers whom we observed were not making much use of alternative possibilities of setting up certain types of group interaction in the creative process or in discussion. The type of communication channel open to the pupil determines the content of what can pass along it. Many of the discussion lessons observed failed miserably not because the teacher had chosen the wrong subject but because he had failed to provide the right communication channel to carry the kind of messages that the subject demanded. The structure of communication networks in the classroom and the teacher's sensitivities to the dimensions of the channels that link the parties concerned are the key to a great deal of the effectiveness of some teachers and the lack of effectiveness of others.

Teachers often look to books or manuals for the secret of effective teaching and they retreat mystically into the notion of the 'born teacher', the individual with a particular type of magnetic personality. 'Pied piper' teachers certainly exist but the possession of such a personality is not the sole key to effective teaching. To master the communication channels between pupils and teacher in the educational encounter is a skill that has yet to be fully explored and developed. The teacher hankering after more stage presence will discover that the 'pied piper' teacher possesses a great deal of such mastery over communication networks.

This completes our overall glimpse of the manifest tendencies reflected in the English teaching that we observed and in the views of the many English teachers whom we interviewed. Using the same categories we shall now go on to examine the manifest tendencies of the drama, fine art and music curricula and that will complete our look at these from the point of view of the teaching function. The section following will deal with manifest tendencies in respect of pupil response.

4   Drama

When we analyse the drama lesson under the same categories that we have used to explore the English lesson a number of very real differences become apparent. Some of these differences reflect important developments in the use of what might be termed the 'art process' in schools. These will no doubt have consequences for the future of arts curricula in general. Unlike English, drama is committed at the outset to an immediacy of response and to forms of direct engagement. This in itself requires that the analysis of drama must be somewhat more probing than for English, if we are to unravel its claims from its real effects so far as the involvement of the pupil is concerned.

1   Self-expression and individuality

If English teachers continually assert the importance of self-expression, teachers of drama take it for granted. Almost by definition educational drama is for self-expression. It is also for direct emotional engagement. Indeed it could hardly be otherwise since the most typical form of a drama lesson is one in which for some part of it the pupils 'simulate' or 'act out' or 'live out' a sequence of events. Without direct expression the exercise has no meaning in drama terms. As one might expect, therefore, the drama teachers we interviewed all recognised the importance of direct sensate engagement in the situation.

Can we conclude from this that the drama teacher has overcome the fears of his colleagues in English departments concerning the dangers of direct emotional release? Certainly not on the basis of our interviews with drama teachers. Because drama teachers are directly involved in the use of emotional response their fears concerning its possible dangers are conveyed even more vividly than in the case of English teachers.

'This is something that really *terrifies* me actually, because I know I'm capable of rousing—I don't know why—emotion in children that perhaps they realise they have got but don't often show to many people. I know I have this ability of getting it out of them if you like which *frightens* me because I suddenly realise what my responsibility is and it *terrifies* me because I don't know if I have the right in a way. This has been something that has been *worrying* me for a while. I don't know if I have the right to wheedle out emotions, but on the other hand they always have a safety factor whereby they can always cut themselves off but I don't know how much in control they are to do that themselves when they've got possibly a stronger personality to battle with I suppose.'

The drama teacher is thus involved in a continuing contradiction between his need to engage the emotional response of the pupil and his discomforting awareness of the dangers of doing this. As with the English teacher it is frequently his sense of responsibility towards the child which dictates his concern. He is afraid for the 'secret life' of the child, the naked terrors and deep-felt needs that might emerge in a social milieu unsuited to coping with them. It is here that we come to the heart of the problem. This same apprehension that so many teachers entertain with respect to emotional expression results from the fact that they tend to see sensate experience in terms of crisis responses. Affective responses for them is perceived as traumatic, as involving gross fight or flight behaviour or ungovernable ecstacy or tearful collapse. Emotional response of this kind does play its part in life but it is neither typical of the ways in which we normally exercise feeling responses nor is its release under conditions of dramatic improvisation necessarily educational or beneficial, although no doubt under some circumstances it can be so.

The cathartic effect attributed to acts of pure emotional release must in any case be distinguished from the complex synthesising of emotional responses into feeling-form. It is this latter process that is involved in the development of an intelligence of feeling. The crux of the matter is this. The gross emotional reactions that many drama teachers are tempted to play with are reactions to the situations themselves. A terrifying situation has the pupils (hopefully) cowering in terror and retreat, and a joyful occasion has them jumping for joy. These gross emotional reactions elicited from the pupils are not necessarily a good basis from which to build feeling-form. Feeling-form, is the product of subject-reflexive action in which the disturbances wrought within the individual are projected in a medium which recalls them. There is no recall involved in emotional responses, however. These are simply subject-reactive. They release themselves in the situation without recall. This is a very important distinction because feeling unlike gross emotional response is a form of reflexive abstraction. Encounters with situations evoke the synthesising of complex clusters of situations in the individual. When my sensate response is subject-reflexive it gives rise to feeling-form. It becomes intelligent. It binds the fragmentary bombardment of sensations into a coherent theme. Crisis situations are often of limited value in encouraging an emotional grasp of the sensations wrought in the individual by such situations. By their very nature they rule out reflexive abstraction because they demand an immediate response, fight, flight, tears or joy, to the situation itself. The individual has little or no opportunity to respond reflexively to the impact that the situation makes upon him. He has his hands full in responding to the situation. The intelligence of feeling involves the organisation of sensate experience as feeling-form, as distinct from emotion as the subjective experience accompanying a gross response of the whole individual to a situation. Since feeling arises from responding (subject) reflexively to sensations wrought within one, the design of situations in drama lessons is of critical importance. Either the situation must itself be such as to permit the individual to concern himself with responding reflexively to the sensory disturbances wrought within him, in which case it cannot be a crisis situation that demands gross emotional response; or if the teacher does use such a crisis situation then he must control its development in a way that introduces artificially the necessary space between the impact of the situation and the action demanded in respect of it so that the process of reflexive abstraction can take place. I shall not pursue this point further for the moment except to point out that when self-expression is understood in terms of the development of an intelligence of feeling (or feeling-form) then the direct and immediate experience of the individual can at last be released from the negative apprehension which surrounds it at present, and take its proper place in our provision for education.

At the moment, however, there is little point in denying that the drama teacher is still very much caught up in the problem of gross emotional responses. It is not surprising that many a drama teacher finds himself behaving like a youngster playing 'chicken' on the motorway, moving into emotional engagement and hoping to sidestep its consequences at the last second. Another complicating factor resulting from gross emotional response is that once emotions are committed in the social situation (and the drama lesson is a social situation like any other) they have consequences for the existing networks of relationships such as those among pupils and between pupils and teachers. As a rule we only commit to a network of relationships the type of emotion or feeling that the network can carry. The drama lesson consists of a simulated network (the dramatic situation) imposed upon a real one (the relationships among pupils and between pupils and teachers). When the simulated network elicits from the pupil an emotional response it can, under certain circumstances, have consequences for the real network that underlies it. The simulated network comes and goes and is replaced with a new and different one. The real network on the other hand is rather more permanent and extends beyond the drama class to encompass the pupil's entire existence in the school. His relationships with his peers and with other teachers are the facts of life with which he must work, must carry on.

Sometimes teachers of drama do operate with dramatic situations that threaten to permeate the barrier between the simulated network (the relationships and the dramatic situation) and the real network (relationships among pupils and between teachers and pupils). They involve the pupils in emotional engagements with situations that are quite real or familiar to them. Some forms of psychodrama attempt this as do some forms of sociodrama. There is no doubt that this is the most potentially explosive form of drama that the teacher may be tempted to initiate because it affects the pupil in his present ongoing situation. It may have direct consequences for that situation with which he is unable to cope. Teachers are very much alive to this problem. The pupils are often alive to it too and may reject attempts to get them to engage in this way. In one lesson that we observed the teacher had got the pupils quite involved in a discussion about phobias. She then set them a highly realistic dramatic exercise in which they explored phobias by imagining that they had a phobia and were trying to tell someone else about it. There was a superficial compliance but a total lack of engagement in the exercise, and it had to be abandoned after ten minutes because of the negative attitude of the pupils. Another time or place or different circumstances might have produced a different response but such a response would then have been likely to involve the pupil in a personal confrontation with which no-one in the situation may have been competent to cope.

It is not only a psychological crisis that can arise when the drama teacher uses dramatic situations in which the simulated network intertwines with the real network. The crisis can be a social one. One teacher that we observed and interviewed worked with a difficult third-year group. The theme was authority relationships. He engaged the pupil's strong feelings concerning these and in a classic rôle reversal situation he had them taking the headmaster to task (imaginatively) in the same form of address as he might have used with them. The teacher suggested the following sentence:

'Look J—(Headmaster) my boy, out of that chair! I'll see you at half-past three and bring with you a copy of the school rules, a pencil, and paper.'

The teacher takes up the rest of the story in his own words:

'Before I finished that sentence half the group were out of the room down to the old man's door and about to charge in— literally they were out, no joke, because they were very up on edge and they feel very strongly about the people with authority in the school. I felt well—do we have the shambles or don't we— hit away—so I quickly nabbed the leader and I said, *"Do we do it properly? or do we have a rabble?"* And *she was edgy so I snatched them back in that moment of uncertainty and we planned.* This maybe was my own fear as a new teacher I don't know but I thought —well they want to do it—and I couldn't divert the energy at that moment—they wanted to go in and tell him, "J—my boy, I want to see you." So we planned it. We got the most "uppity" girl who was really on edge and said, "Now if you go in you must say your piece plainly and clearly—don't go in and gabble else the old boy won't hear you—go in and say it." *She rehearsed her bit* . . . we heard the door go bang—in! She said her piece and the head replied, "I'd love to come but I'm afraid I can't," and *she learned more about social control in those few minutes* than ever I could have spieled about . . . the subtleties were so apparent, "I would love to to come but I can't—I would love to come, I would love to come." '

81

A situation like the one described above indicates the kind of dynamite with which some drama teachers feel compelled to play. It is little wonder that the teacher is obliged to pull back at the last moment and to impose the analytical control that defuses the immediacy of the response turning it into something of an objective act and a calculated risk for the pupil under the protection of the teacher and the 'official' drama lesson. The authenticity of the response died when the teacher (with very good reason) was obliged to stop the pupils from reaching the head's door before they had planned the exercise. This objective analytical planning has nothing to do with the intelligence of feeling. The latter is always direct, it is always feeling.

Many drama teachers avoid this situation by establishing control over the distancing of the simulated network from the real network in the structuring of dramatic situations. Often without consciously realising it teachers determine the process of self-expression and define its limits simply by the selection of dramatic situations that hold the two networks in a certain relationship or at a certain degree of distance. One way of doing this is to ensure that the simulated network is very distant from the real network, that it does not intertwine with the real network. This is one line of defence for the drama teacher. If the pupil's feelings are engaged in terms of situations that are either extraordinary or very far removed from the day-to-day life of the pupil then the possibility of passing off the behaviour as imaginative behaviour, (not for real) has been facilitated. This provides yet another important reason for the extensive use made of wars, natural disasters and other crisis situations in drama. The pupil is encouraged to explore a range of emotional response appropriate to an entirely different situation from the one in which he is implicated in his day-to-day relationships with peers and teachers. Nevertheless this defence on its own is insufficient because although the situation is extraordinary the emotional responses elicited can be real enough, and the teacher walks the tight-rope between the 'legitimate' and the 'non-legitimate'.

As it happens the teacher has yet another line of defence in the great emphasis placed upon discussion and analysis in the drama lesson. Drama is so many things to so many people and arouses so much scepticism on the part of other teachers that the rôle of analysis and discussion becomes pivotal in the drama lesson serving all kinds of purposes from external justification to gratifying the needs of the teacher for internal feedback and for bringing the pupils back to earth in time for the next lesson. Drama teachers are hardly likely to agree with me, therefore, when I argue that this massive prop should be cut down to size and indeed should only ever be used in the full recognition that it can be a serious impediment to the drama process itself. The objective analysis that it yields is entirely subsidiary to the main drama objective which lies in the subjective world governed by the intelligence of feeling. The analytical procedures for *thinking about* disturbances wrought in oneself by situations are not synonymous with expressive action that recalls such disturbances and to proceed as though the two were one and the same is to elude the art process. It is similar to the method used in the English lesson for handling emotional responses in an indirect way. The discussion takes the form of a general analysis of the responses explored in the improvisation in terms of some overall framework in which the necessity and appropriateness of all responses is accepted and individuals are encouraged to accept and recognise the validity of their own responses but at the same time to reflect upon them critically in the light of their *objective* use in the situation. The discussion serves to pull the pupil out of the immediate experience into the world of objective facts in which his own emotional responses figure as objective elements. He is encouraged to consider his own emotional responses and those of others as objective elements in an objective situation. In the end therefore the teacher resorts to the logic of the objective situation as the frame of reference for the emotional experience of the pupil, and the pupil is encouraged once again to objectify feeling. Feelings are always 'acceptable' and 'understandable' given the circumstances but the pupil is encouraged to derive their logic by referring them to the situation and the part they play in it. The logic and order that the teacher seeks to impose upon them is the logic of the objective situation. Intelligence on a subjective level does not enter into it.

It is this period of analysis, in which the objectification of feeling takes place, that many drama teachers consider to be the essential source of validation for what has taken place in the dramatic situation.

'After any sort of emotional upheaval no matter how small or how great there is always an analysis period afterwards, always, always, always . . . yes, always. That's why I put on that other thing—informal discussion and it takes easily 50% of my lesson—and after everything we do we talk about it.'

It is in this discussion period that the whole experience is defused and the pupil is encouraged to confront his feelings in disembodied form, i.e. objectively. The adolescent has a need to objectify his feelings at times and to objectify situations as well, but he also has a need to commit himself and develop his feelings in the situation on a personal, immediate, and subjective level that is quite distinct from the logic of objective situations. He needs to discover in immediate experience the intelligence of feeling that can sustain that commitment and growth of response which translates the individual into the social situation, without compromise, in an act of pure expression. At the point when he is closest to the art process, the drama teacher pulls back to join the mainstream of secondary education which drives the adolescent towards realisation of himself as object among objects. What the pupils paraded in these analyses were not the authenticities of their responses but the meanings they chose to give them in the context of the analysis. This is an altogether different kind of projection exercising a different kind of intelligence.

In so far as the analysis becomes a regular feature of the drama lesson (albeit appearing at the end) and the educational justification for what has taken place, it can serve as an encouragement to pupils on future occasions to bear in mind the objective organisation of responses in the situation *before* determining what their own response will be. This is admirable as an exercise in social control or good social harmony but it is death to the art process, to spontaneity and to the authentic expression of direct (intelligent) feeling in the situation. It is not for nothing that artists have traditionally been suspicious of this kind of analytical discourse. Often it negates the intelligence upon which the art process is built and constitutes an attempt to supplant that intelligence with a rational structure that is quite foreign to the life of the art process.

Despite the fact that the drama analysis and the use of unfamiliar situations by the drama teacher can be used as sources of distortion in the expressive response of the pupil they can also be used entirely constructively as well. The use of imaginative situations that are relatively unfamiliar in terms of the pupil's everyday life may be a vital stimulus to extending and elaborating the emotional tones and contrasts of the pupil's response but only if the process of generalisation in emotional response is carefully monitored by the teacher and the subsequent elaboration leads somewhere. It is possible that objective discussion can also be used constructively provided that the object is to build a real situation for further direct engagement and not to explain away the present one. The art process lives in the curving of the ball as it leaves the hand and not in the trajectory that describes its course. If the actual curving of the ball is not sufficient to the art process then talk about trajectories will not make it so. If the curving of the ball is sufficient then talk about trajectories is unnecessary.

The control of the drama process by its culminating analysis phase leads to the determination of response by objective function. The drama lessons that we observed varied with respect to the amount of distortion introduced into self-expression. At one extreme the action was almost completely built objectively, on the outside as it were, whereas at the other we observed in the work of one movement/drama specialist something that was vital, controlled and filled with the light of the inner act.

2 Control of the medium

Of all the arts in schools drama and movement are the least encumbered with a corpus of techniques which teachers feel they must impart to pupils. Drama has emerged and grown in schools at a much later time than the other arts and its 'youth' is touched with the spirit of the times which is for the relaxing of constraints and the release of personal initiative and expression. Some of the most pressing doubts about the value of what the drama teacher is doing stem from this very freedom, this lack of imposition of formal control. While it is recognised that drama can be enjoyable and self-revealing, many drama teachers themselves are concerned about the issue of whether or not they should seek to encourage and insist upon a great deal more control of the medium by the pupils in order to develop and structure experience more constructively and less wastefully. Without such demands for control of the medium being made upon the pupils the drama lesson is continually dismissed in educational circles as play therapy. This is not to say that drama teachers do not possess control of the medium themselves but that in educational drama there are many doubts about what part, if any, such control should play. Above all the drama teacher is committed to the view that the pupil's expression must not be balked by technical constraints. The drama situation or exercise itself provides a number of constraints and the teacher is often prepared to help the pupil to handle these as and when the need arises.

'The technique grows as it's required—it's easy to give a technique lesson and restful, and it can be quite useful. It may not be. It may be a waste of time because not everybody has the same need for that particular thing to be taught. It is quite useful for the people who are intellectually inclined to know a few scales so that they can handle their movement or whatever it is they're doing within the structure that they have and some of them enjoy doing this, getting to the right spot and making the thing very accurate, and commanding things to make a clear statement. But most of them I find are at the stage where they're just exploring and they are not trying to finish a beautiful thing. . . They want to find out, and they learn as they go along and they may not achieve what they had in fact set out to do. It may take for example a whole term's work for a group of four or five children to complete one concept and they may never actually achieve a thing which they can do, a dance which they can perform, if you like, or a painting that they have painted—even though they will have explored all sorts of areas around it.'

Again we have to introduce an important distinction between rule-directed control of the medium and what I have termed reflexive control. The use of formal techniques, procedures and prescribed ways of doing things are all implied in rule-directed control of the medium. English, art and music teachers are in varying stages of retreat from this form of control of the medium. They perceive formal techniques and prescribed ways of doing things as inhibitive of self-expression if they are not sparingly used. The drama teacher, on the other hand, has tended to reject them from the outset. This means that if there is to be any control at all it will be reflexive control. This involves controlling the medium in process as it were. It can only take place if the individual's awareness can immediately encompass both the sensate impulse and the medium in which idea is built. Somehow all of the magnificent mysteries of the art process are bound up with this phenomenon of reflexive control. Sensate impulse assimilates the medium to itself by shaping its sensory possibilities into a form (idea) that will serve to recall the disturbance to release it. If the impulse is to be discharged then an ongoing guidance system must be established between the sensate impulse and the medium so that as the form grows its possibilities for recalling the sensate disturbance can be effectively realised. This means that the consciousness of the individual must oscillate in an intensive movement between the sensate impulse and the developing form in order to sensitise itself to both independently and to control their vital interdependence. This oscillation of consciousness is a means not only of *assimilating* the medium to the feeling impulse but also of *accommodating* (changing) that impulse to the medium. In other words the form that eventually emerges is not the expression of the original impulse. The impulse itself has undergone modification (accommodation) as has the medium, and the resultant form is the product of their interaction. The medium and the impulse have both 'changed each other' in the process of building the form. This 'changing of each other' and the maintenance of a dynamic equilibrium between impulse and medium is achieved by the oscillation in consciousness between the two. It is this oscillation in consciousness that makes possible the reflexive control of the medium that is fundamental in all art process whether in poetry, drama, music, visual art or whatever.

As the individual (moved by the impulse) begins to shape the medium, the medium itself will exert some influence over the shaping. To the extent that it does so it limits the possibilities for release of the impulse because it imposes something extraneous to it. The impulse itself must therefore undergo some modification to take account of this extraneous element if it is to achieve release through recall. Reflexive control of the medium means maintaining a dynamic equilibrium between the assimilation of the medium to the impulse and the accommodation of the impulse to the medium. That same assimilation–accommodation balance which Jean Piaget sees as characteristic of rational intellectual structures is characteristic of the intelligence of feeling. When reflexive control of the medium is lost either assimilation (of the medium to the impulse) or accommodation (of the impulse to the medium) gains the ascendancy. If it is assimilation that has the ascendancy then the impulse runs riot in an entirely autistic egocentric manner. It gives rise to the richness and instability of fantasy passing backwards and forwards in fragmentary movements into idea and out again.

It slips easily from one idea into another as though it could take on any shape. It is volatile and protean. It does not achieve substantial form and it cannot be held for contemplation. When accommodation has the acendancy then the opposite is the case. The individual accepts the absolute dictatorship of external constraint. He conforms to rule. He copies slavishly. He seeks to create a pre-determined form; one that has been built on the outside of the self. When accommodation has the ascendancy then forms become empty of life, of impulse. When assimilation has the ascendancy then life and impulse are prevented from taking on stable form. Piaget himself has spoken of these states of imbalance in the young child with respect to imaginative play and copying behaviour. He argues that the former is due to an ascendancy of assimilation over accommodation and the latter to the ascendancy of accommodation over assimilation. This is directly comparable to the process described above.

In its extreme form what I have called rule-directed control of the medium involves an excess of accommodation over assimilation in the pupil's response. Similarly, the extremes of the free expression movement involve an excess of assimilation over accommodation. What I have called reflexive control of the medium is the process of maintaining the two in dynamic equilibrium. All three modes of response, rule-direction, free expression and reflexive control are appropriate and essential at different stages of the pupil's development. There is a time for play and a time for copying as well as a time for reflexive control. The importance of reflexive control is that it is the stable, adapted and intelligent mode of response towards which the developmental process drives.

Returning to the drama teachers, it was apparent from our interviews that many drama teachers were intuitively aware of a form of control which was not technique-based and not rule-directed. One teacher of dance expressed the distinction in her own words as follows:

'I don't teach them techniques exactly—this is more contemporary dance. There's a subtle difference, you see. There they have special movements which they must do and this is called technique. And they express themselves through set movements —a bit like ballet except more . . . they teach this in some schools. But in modern educational dance there is no right or wrong movement. *I want them to know whether they're moving slowly or quickly and whether they're moving in space up or down or forwards or backwards.* But within this context they can move as they wish. They can use which part of the body they like whereas if you said I was teaching them a technique I would also be teaching them how to move in movements. I don't ever give them movements and say now this will be the right movement in this situation.'

The nakedness of the drama teacher with respect to developing an adequate level of control of the medium in the pupil is something that he expresses more strongly than teachers of the other arts who can at least fall back upon rule-directed respectability if things get too far out of hand. Drama teachers often feel let down by their training in this respect. They are aware that control of the medium is essential and that this can take place in process, reflexively as it were, and yet the very conditions upon which that control depends are not in themselves the subject of their training. On the contrary, their training takes this control for granted. A few drama teachers do seek to guide and develop the process of reflexive awareness itself and teachers of dance perhaps more so but on the whole there was very little evidence of it in the lessons that we observed. Drama was something of a hit-and-miss affair so far as reflexive control was concerned. Even teachers whose training had convinced them personally of the power of educational drama were not convinced that they were equipped to know what was going on in terms of controlling the medium. One teacher with college training followed by a degree in drama and education put it this way:

'I personally as a new teacher have been well and truly indoctrinated through Slade etc. and I am still really sorting out exactly what I feel about educational drama as this form of therapy cum experience cum whatever. I am more sure about what I feel about the contribution of theatre really. But I'm still thinking of my own experience of going through a sort of practical course of movement, mime and improvisation and so on—that it has a fantastic amount to offer. It has given me—I feel I've gained an enormous amount from it. *But whether I can actually do this for the children I'm still trying to work out. Somebody has been able to do it for me—whether I'm capable of getting on the same kind of wavelength for the children—I don't know.* I'm not sure. Someone did it for me.

89

They succeeded in communicating what they believed in—that is experience in movement and mime working on the principles of persons like Ratovsky and Slade. A particular type of experience, a particular type of learning; a particular type of emotional and spiritual development can take place through these means —they proved this to me, that this can occur, because it's happened to me; but I'm still worried about my own particular ability as a teacher to do it.'

To meet the demands of controlling the medium is still the major problem for teachers of drama in schools. Without adequate means of ensuring that this takes place the intellectually honest drama teacher can lose faith easily and retreat from what he perceives as a world without landmarks let alone criteria or standards.

'. . . a lot of work done in the name of drama is so petty and shoddy. I've been allocated the sixth form to do their "A" Level set plays and this is important to me and I think—at least I can get a chance to work with people who are interested in looking in this particular way at a text, *who are interested in standards, which is a change from the rather amorphous no-standards-allowed world of educational drama.*'

It is not really that educational drama itself lacks standards but it seems that the means for realising them in the teaching situation are not readily available even to those teachers who are taught as specialists.

3 The use of realised form

The use of realised form can take place in two ways in drama, either in the context of performance or of appreciation. On the whole the drama lessons that we observed made negligible use of either. The great majority of lessons used improvisation mime or dance of some kind. Performance is often associated in the teacher's mind with theatre. By and large drama teachers seem concerned to keep theatricalities out of the actual teaching process and to use educational drama in a 'creative' innovative way. Drama work is of course done with plays, usually as an extension of the English examination syllabus, thereby providing an opportunity for the pupils to get on more intimate terms with the texts. Occasionally short dramatic pieces are used for their own sake but this occurs more particularly with the younger pupils. The use of a little musical play entitled *Pawley's Peepholes* from a B.B.C. educational drama series had one of our observers completely enthralled.

In the very few cases where a realised form was used in a performance context in the lessons observed, there was not one in which it was deliberately integrated into work on creative improvisation in the way that a piece of literature or a poem might be used in dynamic inter-relationship with a creative writing exercise. Certainly this may take place but we did not actually observe it, and it is tempting to conclude that it must play a very small part in drama lessons on the whole. Drama's determination to strike out on its own and speak its own truth has tended to make drama teachers suspicious of realised form and of the aura of theatricality that this can introduce. They sometimes use it but apparently keep some distance between realised form and the improvisation exercises in which they engage as though to avoid blurring the distinctions that separate drama from theatre. As educational drama matures this caution will no doubt disappear and the largely creative use of realised form both for appreciation and performance will be possible without sacrificing any of the ideals of creative drama. It will require of course a close relationship, a working together of improvised form and realised form in both performance and appreciation. Such a relationship can provide a vital control in the process of reflexive awareness. As yet educational drama appears not to have developed adequate techniques for achieving this.

4 Personal development

If the English teacher's concept of personal development is often overshadowed by his concept of academic development, the drama teacher has no such haven to retreat to. Drama is hotly defended by its protagonists in terms of the important part it can play in personal development and since it has little or no status as an 'academic' subject it is difficult to see what other justification there could possibly be for it.

The drama teacher's concept of personal development is very much tied to the notion of social adjustment. They perceive the child as moving from the subjective, egocentric world of imagination into the objective allocentric world of rôle-play analysis.

'I think they cease to be quite so subjective—so subjective—obviously you can't do without it altogether, I don't think you'd want to because you'd dispense with the imagination but with the older ones it's different. I do a lot of work in the fourth year with things that they dislike about adults and they can talk about them and think about them and they can do improvisations . . . quite often we don't get to do an improvisation they're so busy discussing in their groups. *They begin to realise that there might be another point of view, that they themselves are growing exactly like their parents, that they are doing the things that they are criticising in adults.*'

The social adjustment theme dominates the drama teacher's concept of personal development. It is a main support for the objectification of the pupil's experience in improvisation that was discussed earlier. Problems of social adjustment are indeed important in adolescent development, and drama has an important part to play here but drama cannot be reduced to this objective or it ceases to concern itself with the intelligence of feeling. Education has yet to recognise that the egocentric response is as vital to maturity as the objective viewpoint. The flight from egocentrism so dominates secondary education, and, furthermore, the status of drama within the school is still so shaky, that drama teachers are often in too great a hurry to lay claim to the social adjustment area of personal development. The rôle play becomes the central exercise for many drama teachers. There is no doubt that drama has a lot to contribute to rôle simulation and furthermore that rôle simulation is one important form of drama. It is not synonymous with drama, however, and a great many of the rôle-play situations improvised in drama sessions in schools have nothing whatever to do with drama although there is no doubt they are a good basis for practical sociology. The richness and imaginative wealth that we find in the young child we are loth to seek for in the adolescent. Over and over again the picture of development emerging from the interviews with drama teachers took the following form:

'When they come up from the junior school there's so much go, so much creative go and they need and use their own ideas alongside what they read, and I suppose you can say that they are being very imaginative. *People say they're very imaginative and we've got to tap the store of creative energy* and so I try to introduce subjects that are going to use this energy and also extend it and then when they become more aware of themselves and think and really do believe they have problems—and they really do have, some of them. I base my work on individuals within the group and try to begin to introduce the reactions of other people besides their own reactions, *try to encourage them to think of other people while they're thinking of themselves*—and later on there are situations that do completely involve other people requiring one to understand people's motives and reactions.'

On the basis of what was observed and what was said in interviews it must be concluded that these drama teachers' concept of personal development was largely restricted to the notion of progressive social adjustment. Those to whom we spoke invariably invoked social adjustment as a justification of their educational rôle when they offered any kind of view of personal development.

5 Examinations and assessment

The pressures concerning the academic curriculum and the institution of formal examinations are beginning to take their toll of drama in schools. As we saw in the case of English, this pressure arises from the community itself and is largely endorsed by parents and pupils. Educational status is strongly tied to the monitoring of the process of behaviour modification (or learning) that is used. There are many conceivable ways in which this process of monitoring, of assessment can take place. The typical academic examination is only one and is characteristic of an educational system which emphasises information storage, culminating stages, and problem 'sets'. The facts, the techniques are all important. We can impress to the extent that we can make statements from which all traces of ourselves have been removed. As my old Professor might have remarked in feigned innocence, 'It is not me who decides "let x equal the unknown variable", and "Venus was observed" means that I am not guilty of observing her which is a good thing because when "*one* is subject to such errors of judgement" then it is just as well that everyone and no-one in particular can make those mistakes.'

The weak position of drama with regard to criteria for assessment places considerable pressure upon drama specialists within the schools.

'I feel there is still a lot of lip service paid to our presence in the school. There's a hard core of the prim academics in the school who obviously feel that drama is way out and not respectable. "It's all this inhibition stuff, all this sensitivity stuff, no standards." We have to put up with that but we don't have to put up with this guilt feeling about it. I'm afraid my relations with the majority of the English department are pretty clapped out which is a pity maybe. It's probably my fault as much as it is theirs, but I feel we have enough support not to feel sort of attacked on all sides. We don't have to get together in a corner and defend our position at every moment.'

The fight is very much on to bring the drama teacher to heel over this issue of assessment. One movement specialist, whose work we found particularly exciting, put it this way:

'Here I'm doing an exam. I've submitted a syllabus, not because I'm fighting for status for the subject within the school but because I feel that the children who are coming up—I don't see why they shouldn't do an exam in it if they want to. Some of them are very good. It's not a thing that happens at the end of the five-year course anyway. They should be able to say, "Well, I do art and movement." *But I think there are more and more art and movement exams creeping* in throughout the country and *I suppose that this is to give the subject some status but it's a mistake I think*. I've written various letters to bodies like the London Guild and so on trying to state my case against examining the subject in an academic way—the whole thing—how it will destroy its contribution to education . . . In a lot of cases I think you're forced into this position, into a tremendous self-defence, defence of the subject, defence of your own aims. Every sort of aggressive attitude I have found myself taking on.'

So far as the problem of academic examinations is concerned the difference as between English and drama teachers is simply that the English teacher is on the inside of the academic system pushing out while the drama teacher is on the outside in danger of being pulled in.

Curriculum structure

The drama lessons that we observed revealed very erratic evidence of internal structuring. Sometimes it was clearly there. More often a situation was selected and the teacher let it grow like Topsy. The use of alternating discussion and improvisation was most certainly a prevalent and recurring feature of the drama lesson. So far as the development of drama curricula throughout the secondary school period was concerned, it was possible to discern a broad structural organisation determined by the teacher's concept of personal development which in many teachers, as was argued, tends to be restricted to the notion of using drama to attack problems of social adjustment. In structuring their courses drama teachers appeared to be trying to meet the problems appropriate to the particular stage of social adjustment that the pupils have reached. For this reason their courses do tend to have an organic structure that relates directly to the personal development of the pupil even though, as I have argued, the concept of personal development is a restricted one.

Curriculum content

I have already covered this to some extent in the section on self-expression. On the whole drama teachers are able to offer an extremely broad range of activities within the drama lesson. Despite the newness of the subject the keen experimental ambience which surrounds drama is highly conducive to innovation and the continual development of ideas and variations on older ideas. In fact drama teachers tend to use up ideas very fast. Despite this fact there are certain recurring themes in what I have called the 'crisis dramas' and also in the 'social problem' rôle plays. If drama teachers are stuck in a rut over content it is not usually because of a lack of availability of ideas but rather because they run into the occupational hazard of getting 'hung-up' on one of these recurring themes, and new content tends to be admitted only in so far as it can be made use of in exercises based on these themes. Content becomes restricted simply because the teacher narrows his definition of drama, usually to some delimited area that he can develop best and also possibly defend more easily within the school. Whether it is contemporary dance, or rôle play, teachers often like to do the drama thing in their own way and specialisation is all too tempting for many.

Mode of encounter

The drama teacher informs the pupils of the name of the game before placing them under starter's orders. After the 'off' he does a little refereeing to ensure that the most basic rules are being observed and that the level of participation appears to be satisfactory. Following that he might name another game and place the pupils under starter's orders again or he might initiate a discussion on what has taken place usually with himself as chairman. More often than not the discussion will in any case take place either then or at the end of the lesson. The mode of encounter is a perfectly straightforward one. The teacher exercises his teaching function most obviously in the preparation and setting of the improvisation or exercise or whatever and in the analysis that ensues later. Many drama teachers prefer not to enter the process once it is actually under way. Their apparent inability to exercise the teaching function during the ongoing dramatic process is in my view a serious blow to the educational effectiveness of the drama lesson. The teacher's task during this process should be to ensure that the pupil remains reflexively in control of the medium and this cannot be done unless there are built-in procedures in the design of the exercise for ensuring that the teacher can detect a breakdown in medium control and indeed can anticipate in advance where it is likely to occur in the exercise. Furthermore he must be able to intervene in the process and help the pupils to restore this control. If the maintenance of reflexive control is the real objective of the teacher then his intervention will not endanger the spontaneous and expressive acts of the pupil. He will help to realise these more effectively. At times he may need to use a little rule-direction or formal technique to ensure that the pupil retains control over the medium. Provided that the real goal remains the establishment of reflexive control then rule-direction can often serve as a transitional stage in its development. In any case drama teachers must soon recognise that the greatest opportunity for entering the drama process educationally is being missed by a great many teachers. By accepting the more modest rôle of general overseer during the drama process the teacher misses the main chance, and the pupils miss the main point.

Communication networks

It is difficult to make generalisations concerning the drama teacher's structuring of communication networks. The very nature of the drama involves him in setting up a number of these in the improvisations that the pupils engage in. So far as the teaching function is concerned, however, he operates at times rather like the hub of a wheel with everything moving around him. At other times he changes over from being the hub of the wheel to being the rim, moving around on the periphery of something going on in the centre. On the whole teachers seemed fairly flexible in their use of these networks. Communication via the rim to the hub is a different communication exercise from that via the hub to the rim.

Perhaps most important of all from the point of view of the managing of communication networks was the general relaxed and open style of communication encouraged by drama teachers. They seemed to ensure that the normal channels among pupils and between teachers and pupils would carry a much richer band of messages than those same channels would carry outside the context of the drama lesson. This added of course to the air of unreality and make-believe which the anti-drama lobby among teachers apparently abhors. The friction between the educational claims of self-expression and academic merit is nowhere more keenly felt than in the establishment by many drama and art teachers of this more open type of communication network. It is all the more threatening to the academic system because it is of necessity a thing of warmth and humour, and as such is all too appealing to teachers and pupils alike in a system that has traditionally managed with a minimum of both.

5   Art

Art lessons in schools reveal a number of important differences, with respect to manifest tendencies, from drama and English lessons. Some of these differences are particularly interesting for the new light that they cast upon the art process in relation to each of the five categories which we are exploring. They help us to recognise that when we talk about such things as individualism and self-expression or personal development or control of the medium or whatever, we need to specify precisely what we mean by them in the context of each of the art processes in which we are interested. A superficial survey of the cultural ethos of the arts in schools might incline us to the view that they all revealed similar tendencies at least in respect of these categories. It is certainly true that there are underlying similarities but it is the differences between them that indicate so much about the possibilities and directions for future development. We might observe, for example, that teachers of both English and drama show some concern for the objectification of feeling processes and for the defusing of direct emotional engagement. The analysis so far has sought to indicate as much. Nevertheless it is also true that the drama lesson explicitly encourages direct emotional engagement as a matter of routine whereas in the English lesson such engagement is something of a rarity. If we are ever to understand the educational encounter sufficiently to develop curricula that are effective in the real situation then it would appear that an analysis of curriculum objectives which probes such differences and similarities is essential.

1   Self-expression and individuality

As with drama and English the teacher of art quite rightly lays some claim to this territory. It would almost be more correct to say that he takes self-expression for granted as part and parcel of what art is all about. Whereas in the case of both English and drama, self-expression is often problematical, especially with regard to direct emotional engagement. In art teachers are not inclined to find it problematical at all. The conveying of personal idea at any level or depth of feeling is considered appropriate to the medium and teachers are on the whole widely tolerant of the types of expression that emerge in the work of pupils. Naturally literal and bizarre images can sometimes occasion comment and concern on the part of the teacher but on the whole the art teacher does not experience the expression of feeling and direct emotional engagement with the medium as either threatening or alarming. He usually takes them as an indication that work is progressing as it should. Among the art teachers that we interviewed we found a very strong consensus that art in schools is very much about the people who make it and only about the things which are made in so far as these are personally expressive of the makers' feeling-idea.

'It's a very personal thing. He's not only putting down what he's seeing, what he's observing. He's also putting down a part of himself that is quite an individual thing.'

The 'part of himself', which the making of the art object is all about, was a recurring theme in the discussions that we had with teachers. Nor was this 'part of himself' restricted by the teachers to 'safe' material. On the contrary art teachers provided considerable freedom for the expression of all kinds of feelings and tended to look upon this expression as healthy and right.

'Emotion is a very crucial and important part of my work. I don't know that I deliberately set out to play on emotion but one finds inevitably that in the work of adolescents there are deep feelings about death and sorrow and joy and happiness which recur again and again—particularly, it seems to me, an absorbing interest in death and things to do with this both with the boys who tend to think of it in violent terms and the girls who see it in more human emotional relationship terms. I think perhaps emotion is very important . . . In the work that we're doing the emotional life of the child comes very much to the fore.'

There are a number of reasons that may be adduced to account for the relative lack of anxiety on the part of art teachers concerning the opportunities that they provide for the expression of feeling. In the first place the art process is a relatively private and individual affair in the context of the art lesson. The individual pupil relates to the teacher in respect of his work but the other pupils are not usually implicated in it unless they are engaged together upon a group project. This means that if 'exposure' does take place it is more likely to be the teacher to whom the pupil is exposed rather than his peers. This is certainly not the case with drama although it is true of creative writing. Another reason stems from the fact that word and gesture (as used in English and drama) are much closer to action in the world than are the elements of form in art and music. Indeed word and gesture make up a large part of action in the world. They are suited to conveying not only our feelings in respect of reality but also reality independently of our feelings. When expression relates the two as it can so easily do with the aid of word and gesture then expression cuts a real path through the world in which we live, tilting at circumstance and contingency, at the heart of objective reality. The pupil's feelings and fantasies can on occasion be experienced as disturbing by the teacher but they may become positively threatening when they appear to be on the brink of translation into action programmes. Words and gestures are closer to the 'brink' in this sense than are pictures or sounds.

The most important reason, however, for the relative lack of anxiety concerning the direct expression of feeling is that although the art lesson traditionally has facilitated the act of expressing feeling it rarely does much to stimulate it or to develop it. Idea and feeling are very personal and very private to the art teacher. He is prepared to help in the facilitation of their expression but tends not to encroach upon the world of idea itself. The art teacher holds up the possibilities of the medium and encourages the pupil to explore them to develop ideas but even in the selection of themes he rarely seeks to pursue the feeling-idea. Themes like 'man-made objects' or 'reflections' allow of the expression of a wide variety of different emotional or feeling responses but they neither directly stimulate nor even require any of them.

The art room is a place where the individual may put a great deal of himself into his work provided he is self-reliant when it comes to feeling and idea. The teacher wants to see emotional engagement but the art lesson is rarely the place where such engagement is actually stimulated as opposed to being passively facilitated. The art teacher tends to be relatively inactive with respect to the pupil's idea, providing a relaxing atmosphere (many art rooms are the most friendly places in the school) and strongly encouraging independence and self-reliance. This demand that the pupil should be self-reliant and independent in the formulation of ideas and should not expect the teacher to involve himself in the process was a recurring theme in the interviews that we had with art teachers.

'I almost bully them after the third year. I say, "I'm not your starting off point any more. You select your starting off point—whatever interests you in this particular sphere. What are the sorts of things that attract you . . ." I want the fourth and fifth year not to need me any more except in a purely advisory capacity when they get absolutely stuck. They mustn't lean on me. I don't want to be leaned on. Anyway they can't lean on people when they leave school.'

The art teacher often sees his rôle as the liberator primarily and as the educator only in a very subsidiary sense. He is there to facilitate liberation of the idea in the pupil rather than to stimulate it directly or to develop it. The atmosphere of the art room is very important in this.

'What I've noticed is the way they come into the room. They loosen up and they come into the room and say Hi! They shout across the room in a way that's very nice. I've noticed that there's a kind of liberating effect as they come in the door, which is what I try to establish because I feel that they've been jammed tight in their desks—fact-fed—and here is a place where at last they can stand on their own two feet; where they are individuals and are able to say, "I've got an idea, I know more or less how to get on with it, and now I must look for what's necessary to get on with it." Therefore it starts with them and not with me.'

Another art teacher contrasting the work done in his department with that done in the rest of the school put it this way:

'They're not used to being asked to think for themselves, to work something out from their own point of view. They're constantly being told things, being given examples which they write down, which they learn and don't relate in any way to themselves . . . I think they've had to put themselves in the background and concentrate on all the information that's fed to them, so that when in the art department we try to encourage them to express their own ideas and feelings they find it difficult to do.'

The manifest tendency that we observed in the art lesson with respect to individuality and self-expression was that both were encouraged in a relatively relaxed atmosphere. However there was little evidence that the art lessons (or the teacher) had a great deal to do with the development of either individuality or self-expression although they provided situations in which development might occur if the pupil's own ideas were already focused and self-sufficient. Because the teachers generally adopted this strongly liberating, facilitative rôle with respect to the pupil's idea rather than an 'educative' rôle it was difficult to escape the view that for many pupils the art lesson served as an enjoyable and welcome release from academic work without much real initiation or development of self-expression. Perhaps the innocent detachment of the teacher from responsibility for or association with the pupil's idea was nowhere better conveyed in our interviews than by the teacher who said simply:

'I wonder a little about the idea of people expressing themselves. I think there should be an opportunity for people who want to say something to do so but people shouldn't be obliged to say something, to make a statement if they don't want to.'

2 Control of the medium

Teachers of art hold ambivalent attitudes towards techniques and control of the medium. Their problem is similar in certain respects to that of drama teachers. They value control of the medium as essential to successful work in the art lesson but they are increasingly suspicious of the inhibiting effects of demanding too much in terms of formal technique. The strong endorsement of the movement towards self-expression and experimentation has led many art teachers to favour allowing the pupil to discover constraints for himself rather than to provide such constraints ready made in the form of techniques. The art teacher frequently takes on a consultancy rôle with regard to control of the medium. If the pupil appears to be in difficulties then he proffers advice but art as discovery and exploration independently pursued is gaining a strong hold as the principal ideology of many art departments.

Nevertheless despite the strong consensus among the art teachers we interviewed concerning control of the medium, a careful look at the work done in art rooms revealed that this was only part of the story. Unlike drama in schools, art has developed within a traditional framework in which formal technique and skilful execution play an important part. Furthermore 'most children have expressed themselves in some form of visual representation from a very early age. Work with crayons, chalks, and paints have been part and parcel of the expressive and communicative acts of the young from pre-school days and these 'offerings' often have the status of 'love tokens' which members of the child's family accept as valid statements. For the child starting secondary school there may already exist a long history of intensive engagement in visual presentations of one kind or another. This may lead the pupil to be increasingly demanding of technique in order to pursue expression more effectively and at the same time it may lead him to be deprecating of free exploration of the medium which has characterised so much of his work in the past. Adolescence brings to the individual the crowning achievement of his development, the vision of the possible. If he is already committed to expressing himself in visual form then this vision of the possible can make or break that commitment depending upon whether the pupil is really able to control the medium sufficiently to explore the possible or whether he is limited to the use of unsatisfactory modes of coping with materials. As one of our teachers explained to her pupils:

'It's not all easy. You have to work hard to produce a certain amount of technical proficiency. You've got to learn how things work. You have to learn that there are certain things which don't do certain jobs. If you want to do a thing properly then you've got to know the right way of going about it—if there is a right way to go about it. If you want to be original and exciting a certain amount of legwork has to be done on your part.'

There is thus a pressure upon art departments to provide sufficient technical guidance and constraint. This pressure arises both from the traditional methods of the art departments in schools and from the demands of pupils. The art teachers themselves are in the dilemma of trying to break from traditional constraints in art teaching, which they feel to be limiting and not conducive to free expression, and yet at the same time to meet the needs of the pupils to control the medium adequately so that they can handle the greater demands made upon expression as a result of adolescent development itself.

There was little evidence in the art departments that we observed to indicate that the dilemma was being solved in a satisfactory manner. On the contrary there was some evidence to suggest that the art teacher experiences difficulty in providing the kind of technical assistance that the pupil needs even when he is aware of what this is. The teacher's problems are compounded by his tendency to pursue technical mastery and control of the medium independently from the work of self-expression. Many an art teacher will happily pursue the problem of controlling media quite formally at an early stage of the course and then relinquish the problem later when the pupil's work is more oriented towards self-expression. It is at this very point, however, that the pupil is most in need of technical assistance, precisely in order to free his expression.

Art is usually compulsory in secondary school for the first three years after which it becomes an optional subject. A not uncommon procedure is to emphasise control of the medium in the early years and self-expression later almost as though the two belonged to different universes.

'What we try to do is to give them a sort of basic design course to begin with and we deal with all sorts of things like colours and textures and so on, and I think if we didn't organise and pinpoint them I don't think it would occur to them to be aware of texture and so forth . . . Once they've done their basic course, by the end of the third year, I try to get them to use their own ideas. I say, "Well now, you've all been just sitting here. I've been telling you what to do. We've all been working away at the same basic problems. Now *I want you to find out what you are particularly interested in and try to work on your own ideas using your own methods.*" You virtually end up with a whole class full of people doing different things and some of them doing pen and ink drawings; painting, drawing from objects in front of them, collages. Someone might be doing a lino cut and someone else busy with some lettering. It's a bit hectic for the teacher but they get a lot more out of it that way because *they put into practice their own ideas and their own ways of doing things*, and of course this is possible because the C.S.E. examination does not tie us down.'

Not all departments organise their curricula in this way. Indeed very many do not. The important point however is that there is a widespread tendency to separate the pursuit of media control from the pursuit of self-expression, and this is a not uncommon way of doing so.

Yet another way of achieving precisely the same unnatural separation between media control and self-expression is to separate out the pupils who want art for self-expression from those who want it for more 'practical' purposes. Perhaps nothing reveals the confusion of the art teacher concerning this problem more than the following account of the way one department that we observed was organised:

'The department is organised in a broad three-way pattern and children in the *first three years* are asked to choose which of the three ways they feel most sympathetic towards and the member of staff who works with that group adopts a teaching approach which we hope is appropriate to the needs of the children within that particular group. The first group is concerned with those children who are interested in communication. They are probably children who are fairly articulate and interested in English—possibly write poetry, maybe interested in Drama and Music. *But the essential thing about that group is that they are concerned with working from ideas and are very much capable of working with limited stimulation and very little directing.* They enjoy exploring their own ideas either individually or in group activity. The second group consists of those children who prefer to be shown some kind of technique or enjoy exploring the characteristics of different materials and I see these children *as those who tend to work rather more intuitively in direct response to material or to activity* rather than to pursue an idea as with the first group. The third group is designed for *those who are looking for a rather more rational clear-cut approach to the teaching of the subject—something that they can recognise as being of value to them possibly*—its actual application in practical terms to real life—some kind of visual communication exercise—possibly some kind of problem-solving situation in which they can recognise that they're being asked to exercise mental faculties to solve problems.'

Not only does this account reveal clearly the separation of the problems of developing control of the medium from the problems of expressing ideas but it throws into sharp relief the 'schizoidal' response of the arts teachers to the pressures under which they are placed in the academic environment of the school. Faced with pressures from pupils and prejudices from teachers and parents, the art departments try to meet a number of incompatible demands upon them without sacrificing their integrity. Within the academic community they seek to stand by individualism and self-expression and not surrender to the class-teaching, fact-learning mode of educational encounter. Nevertheless they recognise the demands of controlling the medium and of exploring it for practical purposes and they find this very hard to reconcile with the ideology of self-expression so far as the actual teaching function is concerned. The pupil's interests and the pupil's ideas have become of very great importance to the art teacher in recent years but he has not in many instances been able to couple the facilitation of these within the context of a teaching situation that adequately meets the pupil's needs for controlling the medium. The result is that art teaching undergoes an unnatural fragmentation which destroys the integral nature of the activity and loses so much of the energy that unity and integration alone can provide.

If we take a closer look at the three-way division introduced into the art department described above we find that the logic of this distinction is rather revealing. The implication behind the designation of the first group would appear to be that it is possible to work from an idea (as a thing of the intellect) which one then seeks to clothe in a suitable material form. The designation of the second group implies that handling material and exploring techniques can take place realistically within the context of a natural response to them in their own right unencumbered by an idea. The third division is simply a recognition of the case for design education. Whatever the justification for such a division of art teaching, it cannot be that the nature of the art process demands it nor that it has any real basis in the psychology of the pupil. Art is not the finding of a jacket for an idea nor is it the mindless manipulation of materials.

The teachers of the art department above would be horrified to hear this division characterised in those terms, but that would appear to be the naked logic behind it although in practice it was variously interpreted. The point is that the fragmentation which takes place with respect to art in schools follows the 'fault lines' of the academic system rather than the needs of the pupils or of arts teachers. It is interesting to note that the three-fold division that we have discussed does have such a basis within the academic system.

Formulating ideas and then clothing them in a suitable and acceptable way is an important part of the work of English departments and liberal arts within schools and to some extent the humanities also. Developing adequate techniques for problem solving in a practical and material sense takes in the *modus operandi* of the sciences, crafts, and technological subjects. Working from a direct and immediate response to visual material fulfils needs internal to the art departments themselves.

In dealing with the pupils processed through the academic system, arts departments have the greatest difficulty in meeting the school with a unified approach. Fragmentation of the art process is the price that is paid for preserving some integrity in the art department but fragmentation is often self-defeating because it is so costly in terms of the creative energy of the teaching staff who for much of the time are working with groups engaged on anything but the art process. Furthermore such fragmentation hinders opportunities for the pupil to develop control of the medium and to express himself. It also leads to a compartmentalisation of art that matches the compartmentalisation to which he has been conditioned throughout his academic career, namely that there are different universes made up of ideas (mental), materials (physical), and techniques (practical). The realisation of this was not lost on the head of the department which employed this division.

'My worry about it is that perhaps the children are thinking too much in one kind of way. One hopes that one is building upon the strengths and the interests of the children, but one has to go through a good deal of questioning. It is difficult to be sure in one's own mind whether the boy who would naturally tend to choose the problem-solving practical approach, *who tends to be interested in physics and chemistry and that kind of activity in the school might not get some benefit when asked to work in some very poetic sort of way which is against his nature but which in the long run might do him more good*—one doesn't know—it's a sort of dilemma one is in; at the moment I feel I want to build on children's interests and on their strengths and the things they're interested in.'

It is apparent from the above quotation that the division of activities within school has quite consciously influenced the formulation of this department's policy. Art does not easily admit of such distinctions, however, and in practice some very good work took place simply because they were not always adhered to and in any case were variously interpreted by teachers and pupils alike.

It is important to note that although this division had a particular academic philosophy behind it, there is a similar kind of distinction widely used by art teachers and justified by them in art terms. Many teachers prefer to work from materials to 'impulse' (i.e. the individual's feeling experienced as impulse) on some occasions and from impulse to materials on others. In the art process this two-way oscillation has to take place in any case and control of the medium is hardly possible unless the artist's consciousness can move in both directions. This particular distinction is very important for the achievement of self-expression because it facilitates the very making of idea through media control. If this is to happen then the oscillation from materials to impulse and back again must take place continually in every piece of work that the individual does. Whether we start with the materials or the individual's 'impulse', is of much less importance. Self-expression is compounded of material and impulse indivisible, fused. Together they make up feeling-idea, form. The idea does not exist before the form (not the art idea) and the material does not attain form without impulse. We often talk as though idea became *expressed* in material form. This is entirely misleading. Idea is made in the interaction between the individual's feeling, experienced as impulse for release, and the medium which he works into the form that releases it.

It would have to be concluded on the basis of what was observed that art teachers tend to organise their teaching in a way that introduces an artificial distinction between idea for expression and material for manifestation. Control of the medium is hindered by such a distinction because the living contact between the two is easily lost and with it the pupil's respect for his own work.

3 The use of realised form

Very little use is made of established 'works of art' as an integral part of the creative activities of the pupils. In fact we observed nothing approaching creative appreciation. Art appreciation and art history do appear with examination classes but they are usually approached in essentially the same academic way as syllabus texts for English. No doubt art appreciation properly integrated with creative work plays an important part for some teachers but it was non-existent in the work that we observed nor was it mentioned by the teachers whom we interviewed.

Exhibitions were mentioned, however, and it was apparent that art teachers were occasionally concerned to introduce the pupils to the works of the masters where visits to art galleries were feasible or even to mount exhibitions of a more minor nature within the school. In neither case, however, is this usually an integral part of the work of the department and teachers are often frustrated and disillusioned by the negative response these exhibitions apparently receive from the pupils. Concerning exhibitions in the school one teacher put it to me this way:

'I should have got exhibitions around by now but I'm frightened. I've had too many things damaged. If you put decent things out they're rather inclined to pencil human pubic hair on and things of that nature, on something that you really value, something of your own perhaps, and when it's not your own you've got to be really careful—you don't want glass cases all over the place, besides there is no room for them. So I would say it plays very little part.'

It is hardly surprising that this kind of response is common when the great wealth of the art world achieves no integral place in the creative work of the art departments themselves and yet teachers are continually surprised and often secretly furious with their recalcitrant barbarians whose own work they may have praised or found worthy in the past:

'I must confess to a certain amount of dismay when I am faced with people with a very superficial or immature approach to the work. I know this is a personal weakness that I am continually fighting. I took ninety pupils to an exhibition of Indian Art *for half an hour*. I felt a certain sort of regret—I mean this was a trivial thing really—I felt a certain sort of regret *that children can be so utterly illiterate as to pass by things which really are tremendous master-pieces without even a second glance*. One knows that one is exposing children to these things and one hopes that at some time in the future this experience will be remembered and have some kind of impact upon them. But the experience for me is tinged with a certain amount of regret that they aren't mature enough to be able to appreciate, to even begin to appreciate, what they're being exposed to.'

This teacher, who was deeply considerate of the pupils and always interested in their view of things, was not being in any way a culture snob in making these remarks. He cared for what the pupils felt, and he was hurt that what touched him deeply should leave them cold. He was merely expressing the discovery felt by every teacher who holds up Art in its sacred form to be profaned by the gaze of the indifferent class. Whether it is Dickens or Haydn or Rembrandt, the pupil has little respect for what he cannot use and he cannot use anything that he has been inadequately prepared to contact in experience. Such preparation, if it is to be really effective, requires that works of art be given a dynamic relationship to the consciousness of the pupil as it evolves in the creative process.

4 Personal development

Art teachers encounter the problem of personal development in a very interesting aspect so far as the curriculum is concerned. This aspect centres upon the adolescent's problem with respect to control of the medium. Although it appears with all of the arts it tends to be partially obscured by other factors in drama, creative writing, and music. In art it takes the form of what I term the 'representational crisis' and it is in this form that it is particularly obvious to anyone who is around to observe it. Before we come to the representational crisis however it will be as well to look at the general picture of personal development as it comes across to the art teacher. The following is a fairly typical account.

'The first years, especially the first two, are really smashing. They're lovely—especially the little boys—they're all sort of keen and inquisitive. The little girls are a bit shy on the whole, and then they sort of get into the swing of the school and they become a bit rowdy but none the less enjoyable, they enjoy things and it's terrific to work with them. In the third and fourth years they quieten down and become a lot more inhibited. They tend to be a bit drab. I enjoy working with the fifth and sixth years because they talk a lot—you can hold an ordinary conversation with them, you can enjoy their company—they're interesting as people.'

It is the change that takes place in the third and fourth years (chiefly) that is particularly important for what I have termed the representational crisis. Adolescence alters the most fundamental aspects of the individual's relationship to reality. The most important development is that he comes increasingly to accept the real world as only one possibility among many, whereas before, the world as he knew it was the only possibility. Intimately bound up with this development is a gradual separation, in the consciousness of the adolescent, between the object on the one hand and the symbol or form which refers to it on the other. The young child treats words and pictures as though they were part and parcel of the universe to which they refer. He behaves towards an object as though it could tell him its name if he listened hard enough. During adolescence, however, the individual increasingly recognises that the symbol and the representation belong to a different universe from the object itself, that objects are given names and are represented by acts of the human consciousness. This discovery immediately involves the individual in a new problem. If the symbol or form is truly distinct in origin from the object, if they arise in different universes, then how adequate is his form, his picture as a representation of the object? This is the basis of the representational crisis. It is less apparent in the case of words, because words are arbitrary symbols learned and used by adults and children alike and the problem of alignment between word and meaning is less obvious for this reason. With pictures, however, and other representative forms, the individual becomes increasingly concerned by their divergence from the object. He wants to be able to make them resemble the object and he judges his representations as failures when they do not do so.

'They become much more critical of what they do by the time they're in the fourth year. And this makes them much more inhibited in what they're doing and much less willing to tackle anything. They sort of sit and say that they can't do things and when they do it's hard, and they begin to judge what they do by outside standards, by—well in terms of pictures they've seen or books and things like that. I find I need to encourage them more and, in a way, *to help them more in the sense of actually teaching them techniques. They become very interested in these.*'

Although it was apparent from our discussions with art teachers that they did not fully understand the representational crisis most of them were clearly aware of it and did respond to it in their teaching in certain ways. Often they attributed the crisis to the developing awareness of the pupil in general. As another teacher put it:

'Round about thirteen they're much more aware of the visual stuff they see around them, adverts and comics and things like that, and they want their work to look like it and well—say a class of thirty—maybe two of them can get their work to look like that and the rest can't because maybe they just don't have that natural facility.'

Sooner or later most art teachers confront this problem in one form or another. Their response to it has very important consequences for the teaching of art in schools. In fact part of the solution to the problem of the representational crisis that is favoured by art teachers is suggested by adolescent development itself. As a result of his new-found capability of reaching towards the possible the adolescent's involvement with abstraction and symbolic reality as opposed to concrete reality takes on a new dimension. As the real becomes only one among a number of instances of the possible he looks with increasing interest at possible reorganisations of the elements of the real, at abstraction itself. The idea of exploring new organisations and possibilities now appeals strongly.

This reaching for abstraction provides a paradoxical balance to the associated movement in consciousness which makes the adolescent concerned about the 'likeness' between his visual representations and reality. In other words precisely at the point where he wants to copy the object exactly, he ceases to believe in the integrity of the object and is prepared to reorganise it. The art teacher perceiving this development intuitively frequently chooses this point in time to lead the pupil into working in terms of abstractions as a way of solving the representational crisis. It is as though he were saying 'You can't draw objects because you haven't got the skill but soon you will realise that objects can be broken up and you can make pictures without them and express all sorts of ideas.' That this is not an unfair indication of the way in which many art teachers go about solving the representational crisis can be seen from the following quotation from an interview with the head of an art department:

> 'Round about that stage [third year] we're giving them completely different things to think about. We aren't requiring them to draw things because you only get the response "I can't draw" so they won't do it. So what we tend to do is to get them to decide on some abstract theme.'

The problem with the solution adopted explicitly by this teacher and implicitly by many others, is that it is no solution at all. In trying to use the movement towards abstraction in the adolescent's thought to counteract the representational crisis, these teachers are shelving the representational crisis rather than solving it. The result is simply that the abstraction process itself is undermined so far as art is concerned. The author believes that the solution of the representational crisis is a prerequisite to an adequate level of functioning on an abstract level. The pupil who is unable to attain representational control *or insight* at some level of competence is unlikely to be able to create effective abstractions. If he is to retain sufficient control over the medium as he moves towards abstraction then he will at least have a grasp of the nature of representational control on an immediate and personal level. Without this the forms he creates can become empty and externalised, art jackets for intellectual potatoes. If the pupil is to retain his respect for the things he makes then his needs for control of the medium must be gratified rather than shelved. Abstraction as a high level of functioning is indispensable to the art process in schools. Abstraction as a means of shelving the representational crisis is self-defeating and destructive of the art process.

5 Examinations and assessment

Because he is already caught up in the trappings of the formal academic examination, the art teacher is decidedly more uncomfortable than the drama teacher on this issue of assessment. He feels the absurdity of his position vis-à-vis the academic examination very keenly indeed. The impetus of art teaching in schools is committing it to move in a direction which is largely incompatible with the goals of the academic examination. The product, the result, the standard reached, are becoming a less important basis for assessment, for many art teachers than was formerly the case, and yet these teachers need to assess and monitor the pupil's progress is as great as that of others. Indeed in some respects it is greater because by emphasising process rather than product the teacher has moved into an area where the intangibles are so many that they threaten his security. Teachers need to assess the pupil's progress if for no other reason than to assess their own. Without some sort of monitoring system they would soon be lost, and this thought was certainly not lost on the art teachers themselves.

'I don't think one can assess the value of one's work in terms of the actual work that's produced. You've got to evaluate it in terms of much more intangible things than that, and this is very difficult and may depend very much on one's own mood . . . there's sort of no real way of saying well this is right and the other is wrong; it's all very intangible. *This can be quite frightening and so much so that I think well now today I'm going to—they're going to do this and I'm determined to get things and results just so that I can know where I am.* There comes a point when you can no longer sort of think—"I want to know how the children are getting on," you're concerned about "How am I getting on?"'

Art teachers frequently establish a more intimate relationship with the pupils in respect of work produced than many of the teachers of academic subjects simply because of the very personal nature of the work. This more intimate level of pupil–teacher communication in respect of work produced can result in the teacher perceiving the examination as a somewhat irrelevant intrusion which threatens to destroy the 'meeting of minds' between teacher and pupil.

'I'm not sure but I don't think examinations are the best method of assessment. You see, from the fourth year upwards it becomes much more intimate between the teacher and the pupil. I'm beginning to learn more about them and their needs and they're beginning to learn more about me and what I feel about things and if we can make an amalgam between what I feel and what moves me and what moves them then we can come together in a very much more intimate relationship.'

These two extracts from different interviews illustrate very well the ambivalence of arts teachers generally towards examinations and assessment. Assessment itself appears to be essential to the sense of security of the teacher but examinations of the formal academic type are a mockery of everything he is trying to achieve. They are more than this in fact because they can positively interfere with the establishment of his own objectives. It is for this reason that art teachers to whom we spoke enthusiastically embraced the advent of the C.S.E. as producing a form of assessment that was at least intelligible to them.

'C.S.E. a great improvement! Much more valuable. The fact of an examination is a bit of a limitation I suppose. You're always finding yourself saying, "Well it will be nice when the exam is over." Certainly the new C.S.E. examination seems to me really rather exciting.'

The very nature of the art process as conceived of by teachers will lead to an increasing pressure for the kind of control over the criteria of assessment that is implicit in the C.S.E. principle. By this means teachers will seek to bring the form of assessment much closer to the realities of teaching art in school and much closer to the personal development of the pupil. What has clearly emerged from our interviews is that the need of art teachers to assess progress in the pupils is as great as that of teachers of academic subjects. The machinery required for doing so, however, must needs be infinitely more complex and subtle than that of the academic examination.

Another dimension to this problem is provided by the increasing emphasis being given to design education in schools. Many art educators in seeking to strengthen the position of art in schools have embraced the design education movement with great enthusiasm. Design education does have an important part to play in art curricula. It is by no means a central point, however, and the great prominence it achieves in places is at the expense of the art process. Whenever it represents an attempt to accommodate to the academic system and to justify the art process by the achievement of measurable results, it usurps the educational function of art making. When this is the underlying motive, the art lesson makes virtually no contribution to the development of an intelligence of feeling. All too often what people mean by visual literacy is the development of objective standpoints from which to treat sensation. The art process is always in the greatest danger from such objective standpoints. It so easily degenerates into something else altogether and since the greater part of the educational system is already devoted to ministering to that 'something else', an art world that is going over to design education is merely contributing to the imbalance.

Curriculum structure

There is little now that can be said concerning curriculum structure. Considerable attention is paid to the structuring of the art curriculum but the basis for this structuring is extremely variable. It is partly a response to the 'respresentational crisis' mentioned earlier, partly to the pursuit of art for examination purposes and partly to some theoretical notions that an art teacher himself may have concerning the way the course should be structured. The result is that many art departments appear to lack what one might term a coherent educational policy and even where a definite structure has been superimposed it appears strangely irrelevant to the developmental needs of the pupils.

Curriculum content

The art lessons that we observed did not reveal as much imaginative use of content as one might expect. Art teachers were frequently very staid and conventional when they were stipulating particular exercises for the pupils to work on and the ubiquitous Christmas cards and thumbpots were a little depressing. The selections of themes were usually of a very general nature, e.g. 'reflections' or 'man-made objects', and the teachers expected the pupils to produce their own ideas. The teacher often did introduce the pupils to novel ways of using materials but many teachers whom we interviewed seemed to be anxiously on the lookout for these techniques as though they perceived a distinct shortage of new ideas constantly looming. In questioning us some of these teachers openly indicated that what they expected of a curriculum development project were tips of the 'new kind of lantern show' variety. The art teacher would certainly be in less of a rut over content if he did not so easily separate the world of 'idea' from that of 'materials'. By leaving the ideas to the pupil he finds himself keeping his end up by hunting around for materials in a somewhat confused if not 'mindless' way.

Mode of encounter

The mode of encounter between teachers and pupils within the art lesson is modelled on that of the art college. Essentially the teacher spends a great deal of time dealing with one individual at a time. He may set the task or whatever by addressing the class as a whole but then he passes from one pupil to another commenting on the work in progress and offering advice when it is required. The mode of encounter is such as to reinforce the private and personal nature of the activity and to encourage the self-reliance that is a characteristic concern of art teachers. The pupil is essentially on his own but able to consult the teacher if need be. The problem is that the teacher is often unable to enter the process at the point between the pupil's feeling-impulse and the medium he is working in. Provided the pupil remains in control of the medium there is no problem but when that control is lost then the teacher may find it very difficult to restore it simply by offering advice. The fact is that unless the pupil's work is explicitly phased in advance by the teacher in such a way as to permit the teacher to monitor the process of controlling the medium and to enter the process at particular stages delineated in advance, he will be unable to exercise the teaching function in a meaningful way. This phasing of the pupil's work in accordance with some clear objective in terms of feeling-idea means a great deal closer teaching than most art departments are accustomed to.

Communication networks

The art teacher uses the traditional network of communicating with the class as a whole but communication between himself and each individual takes up a very great deal of his time. Group networks among pupils themselves are becoming an increasing part of the final communication structures as art teachers initiate more and more group projects. As with the drama lesson the relatively informal nature of the communication channels themselves encourages quite a rich interchange of messages. It is a fact that many art rooms are pleasant places to be, either on one's own or with others.

6 Music

Of all the arts that we have looked at in schools music is apparently in the greatest difficulties. Despite a long and in places impressive tradition, it repeatedly fails to obtain a general hold on the musical development of the majority of pupils and is considered by many pupils to be irrelevant to anything that really concerns them. Achievements with choirs and orchestras made up of the 'musical minority' brighten the scene here and there, providing sustenance and balm for the class-weary teacher. However, this gratification is relatively short-lived, and the teacher must sooner or later face the fact that in all probability he has not found the secret of making music a fulfilling experience for other than the 'musically inclined' minority of the pupils. Everything seems to conspire to make the situation of the music teacher as difficult as it can be. He is balked by prejudice on the part of both staff and pupils alike. He is inadequately resourced and must continually listen to complaints about noise but, perhaps most serious of all, his training does not usually equip him to deal with music for classes in an effective way nor does it encourage him to exploit the wide variety of possibilities for music making already developed in *avant-garde* centres, for use in schools. The music teacher is often condemned to work out his existence in the secondary school as the martinet on the other side of the music stand, hiding his own sensitivity to protect it from further abuse and thrusting the rudiments down reluctant throats. He does his duty grimly like a soldier in an unpopular war, 'the unwilling doing the unnecessary for the ungrateful'. Often he loves music too much to be happy about it.

1 Self-expression and individuality

Music teachers actually laid very few explicit claims to developing individualism and self-expression when compared with the teachers of the other arts whom we interviewed. They seemed to respect the right of the individual to respond in an individual way to music and they frequently emphasised the rôle of fun and enjoyment in the music lesson. The music teachers felt that the actual making of music should be fun but their training continually constrains them to retract from this in practice.

'Essentially it should be enjoyment I think, practical music should be enjoyment. *I'm talking about non-academic music obviously*. It should be enjoyment first of all. It shouldn't be a drudge or a drag or just another lesson that they go to and sit rigidly at desks and work the next fifteen pages of an exercise book.'

As this teacher says, however, he is talking about non-academic music and in fact in many schools academic music is all there is. Notational analysis, musical theory, the lives of the composers and the National Song Book is still the main course served up for a great many children, and while the content is varied many teachers still retain the basic structure. Music teachers who stand out against this have the whole weight of a profession heavily armed with traditional practice to fight against. One teacher who was deeply committed to involving the pupils and achieving some level of self-expression put it this way:

'The problem is trying to put over my point of view not to the children but to the music adviser. I went to a meeting and there were twenty-two music teachers there. Only two of us thought that music lessons should not be formal and should not be alien to the experiences of the children and so I suggested to the meeting that those children who were to stay on at school next year should be encouraged to write the music that means something to them, protest songs, and pop songs perhaps. Well, the older ones looked at me in absolute horror. If these children were to stay on then they should do C.S.E. music and they should learn their music in the traditional way.'

What does 'learning their music in the traditional way' actually mean? The head of a music department put it to us this way:

'The conventional idea still prevails that it is really only necessary to teach the lives of the composers, a bit of elementary harmony, to be able to sight-read music and to be able to sing nicely in a choir.'

One of the problems is that the music teacher is usually himself trained from the point of view of the instrumentalist. The disciplines and constraints of learning a musical instrument, being able to read what a composer has written and knowing enough about theory to analyse the piece properly constitute the outlook upon music that has influenced the teaching strategy of so many teachers. For them music has always existed in the form of set pieces which are there to make demands upon them in order to interpret them and bring them to life. Music teaching is therefore defined as the attempt to discipline pupils to sing or play a set piece properly or to listen to a set piece properly. There is among music teachers a fear and distrust of experiment, of musical invention, of anything that threatens the disciplined service to the musical masters that their training has developed in them.

More than any of the arts with which we have dealt, music in schools is about the enactment of ideas. The music teacher's training is not dominated, as is that of the art teacher, by the problems of making ideas. He is concerned to represent or enact ideas that have already been made, even allowing for the fact that he adds something of himself in the enactment. It is difficult to overestimate the profound consequences that this fact alone has for the entire response of the pupils to musical experience in schools. Since music in schools is rarely about making ideas the pupil's need to participate creatively, to add something of himself, is gratified only to the extent that he can master the enactment of the musical ideas of others sufficiently to interpret them. Enactment is essentially a process of representation. It involves an excess of accommodation over assimilation. The external form is master. The pupil confronts real problems in trying to meet demands for accommodation at this level. In the first place such accommodation is simply not possible if he has not previously been able to assimilate musical 'ideas' to his own sound-making activities. The process of assimilation is akin to the process of play. He must literally be able to play with sounds. Since the entire skill is an accommodatory one this assimilatory component will usually take the form of a natural facility to work and play with sound. The music teacher quite naturally feels drawn to pupils who have this facility and he easily despairs of those who do not. In a strange way he is right, for as long as music teaching in schools is led from the point of view of the instrumentalist he is merely reflecting intuitively the fact that people who cannot 'think sound' cannot represent it other than mechanically. All too often the music teacher finds himself forced to initiate this process of mechanical sound-making to the intense distaste of himself and the pupils. Without feeling, music is dead, and no-one knows this better than the music teacher. The question that he asks, quite naturally, is what is he to do to get pupils to play music when they do not have this natural facility. We shall have more to say about this in a moment but we can at least point out that a great opportunity is being missed for creating the conditions in which playing with and assimilating sound forms to the pupils' own sound-making activities can more easily take place. Many teachers who know that this must eventually happen also know that their own traditions and training are the greatest impediment to bringing it about.

'One of the great problems is the fear of the teachers to jettison their skill and to enter a classroom "naked and unashamed". Now that I've done this I feel my field of music is widening and I am becoming a better musician all the time and less dependent on the so-called props of music. *I find now I am quite happy to make music while just walking along; making up a blues rhythm with my feet.*'

This teacher certainly realised the nature of the problem, and there is some reason for hope where teachers make the same discovery and actually bring it to bear upon the teaching situation. It must be pointed out however that not long after our interview this teacher gave up teaching music altogether and took up a part-time post teaching Latin in another school. He is himself a fine musician who could not reconcile his discovery with the constraints of teaching music in schools. It is sad that in this case a man's enlightenment must mean his exit from music teaching. Speaking of that enlightenment he says:

'Musicianship, the language of music, phrasing, all these improve. My technique does not. I don't do sufficient practice. I am a better musician *per se*: not executant. The feeling for music is the better since I have abandoned the call to be an exponent as opposed to this "living the musical experience and creating it unhindered by standards or props". I am a man who found that the subjects he was teaching the children were virtually irrelevant to their development. I question the whole value of the academic structure.'

This 'call to be an exponent' and the demands it makes of teachers and pupils alike is the chief contributing factor to the virtual murder of musical experience that takes place daily in our schools. The most immediate and expressive of all the arts is the most separated from immediacy and expression within the teaching situation. Here and there however one can discern the self-expressive aspect emerging in the work of teachers who are experimenting tentatively with a different kind of model before them. Instead of depending upon the ideal of the exponent, the instrumentalist or vocalist, there is the living growing creative spirit of the makers of music to guide them. Dropping the props is not easy. Those trained as exponents are unsure of where the work is leading. They have not been used to trusting their intuition while exploring unknown parameters. So much of their own training has been devoted to detecting deviance of one kind or another that they have come to take the norms and assumptions of music very much for granted. Indeed they accept them as categorical imperatives which require no justification other than to assert them within the technical syntax of musical language. When the music teacher is not hunting the deviant, the note off-key or whatever, he is easily lost. It is one thing to appear 'naked and unashamed' but it is another to freeze to death as a result. Without some guidance and curriculum development many music teachers would lack sufficient confidence in the teaching situation to sustain them without props. Nevertheless many of them are trying to make a start on this. Creative music is increasingly playing a larger part in schools although the teachers' ideas about it are often a little raw and aimless at present. However, step by step they are gaining confidence from their experiments.

> 'Sometimes if I'm doing a small piece with a class I don't just leave it at singing—we don't have much in the way of equipment but what I have got I just sprinkle around. They say, "Well, what do you want me to do, sir?'—I say, "Anything you like— listen to it then rap away on a drum as to what you think is right for this particular piece of music." Nine times out of ten the correct sort of rhythm will come out however primitive it might be . . . they'll listen to the beat, they'll listen to the

speed of the music and then without me having shown them any thing, not even how to hold the instrument or anything, a rhythmic pattern will come out. *This isn't me telling them; it's them you know— "You've got the instrument. You play it! You do what you think ought to happen!"* '

Nevertheless we must not see this kind of experiment out of perspective. Many teachers are dipping their toes in the water and are a long way off plunging in, let alone starting to swim. It would be misleading to assume for example that the work described above is integrated in spirit into the structure of the music curriculum as such. 'Executant' music maintains its grip on the curriculum despite such experiments. The teacher quoted above gave the following account of how he organises his music lessons.

'I divide lessons up into three. We have a singing period which also incorporates any instrumentalists, *any people who are good at musical instruments—they can show us what they can do* . . . when we do that we do songs that we've already previously learned so that we don't spend time learning the notes, the words, etc. I then have a period where we learn a new song so that in future lessons we can, as I put it, tart it up—you know, with all the added instrumentation. Finally we have a listening period. Sometimes I allow music of their own choice. They say why they brought it, why they like it and so on. I bring a piece of music and say why I like it . . . then we talk about it.'

Even working with this fairly straightforward and, one would have thought, entirely respectable if not conventional framework, this teacher is still looking over his shoulder at the pundits and reflecting in his own mind upon the extent of his deviance.

'This isn't altogether desirable and not what the textbooks on music teaching say you should do but I find it works.'

With so many laws and so many musical sentinels to enforce them it is little wonder that the individual teacher can feel at times that even the slightest deviation is treason.

2 Control of the medium

As we have seen, control of the medium is central to the whole general outlook of music teachers. Indeed with some music teachers it is almost an obsession. Nevertheless control of the medium has a somewhat different meaning for the music teacher than for the art or drama teacher. On the theoeretical side music teaching still resembles the largely defunct traditional approach to the teaching of English language from the standpoint of grammar, while on the practical side techniques and formal standards abound. Medium control in terms of creative awareness, in terms of the reflexive oscillation between impulse and the medium (other than on the level of the skilled instrumentalist) is as assuredly absent as the syntax and techniques of the exponent are present. When it comes to creative work in music then you have to be one of the twice-born initiates. The music teacher will often allow that the unlearned may create in art or drama but to suggest that he may do so in music is to utter an obscenity. As our music teacher lost to the profession put it:

'Training colleges are run by very good musicians. In a local college, no names, a group was formed of people just interested in creativity. They met to experiment in the home of this teacher and were very happy doing things that they had never done before (clay modelling, art work and the like). They then asked to move on to music and his reply was, "I cannot make music with people who cannot play a musical instrument!" Now you can get a group of people who are keen and you can give them table knives and forks and within half an hour you can produce quite a good composition of music—every bit as good as you can do with clay modelling. But the teacher training colleges I have seen have no conception of getting down to this which is a very important matter.'

This awe with which music teachers surround their skills creates very real barriers keeping a great many potential music lovers from ever coming to grips with the medium. An art teacher that we interviewed was trying to introduce relationships between visual material and sound and reflected rather gloomily on 'this question of skills':

'I know from my own experience that there was within myself this tremendous desire to be able to express or communicate or say something in sound but the skills of instrumental playing and reading music and so on are such that *for me personally they become an impossible barrier; and I'm sure that this is equally true of a lot of children that I'm teaching.* There is a desire—and there could be a tremendous sensitivity towards the use of sound which somebody ought to be developing.'

Music teachers are certainly not unaware of this problem and many of them make real attempts to try to overcome it but they often fail because they are merely disguising technical demands in a way that makes them appear more palatable rather than overcoming the need to make these demands. One music teacher suspicious and disaffected from the formal music teaching scene despite her traditional training, resisted picking up this particular chestnut:

'One of them (musical advisers) said, "You can make this teaching of note values a lot of fun.' I thought, "Yes! by experimenting with calling a crotchet an apple and such like changes or juggling of nomenclature yes I could!" But then I thought—"Even teaching them this way—so what! There's better things to do with the time . . ." This chap said it was discipline of the mind to do formal music.'

I have myself marvelled at the wizardry of some of the crotchet-to-apple transformations that musical educators are now dreaming up. However, I am convinced that it is a change of heart rather than a change of clothes that is needed. All too often the change of clothes is initiated for the wrong reason, namely that children don't need music for any instrumental value and they must be cajoled into participating.

'Of course, I mean in a subject like Maths or Geography you can hold it over their heads that they have to know these things to get on; but in music if you have it too strict you don't get any response.'

Disguising the 'strictness' of music in an orgy of crotchet-to-apple transformations is no better and no worse than teaching children to draw by numbers. Sooner or later music teachers must recognise that there is no substitute for an active and spontaneous engagement with musical experience engendered by the pupil's sense of its relevance to him personally and his capacity to realise himself in musical idea. The opportunities for providing pupils with a rich assimilatory basis for building musical ideas of their own and appreciating those of others is largely being lost. The existence of the Orff-type toned percussion instruments makes possible a whole world of experiment for relating sound to impulse and producing musical idea. The ease with which these instruments can be mastered frees the child without natural facility to play with sound and idea in a way that might even be used to build a real basis for the more accommodatory act of playing a musical instrument, always assuming of course that this is considered desirable. The point is not, however, that children should become instrumentalists but rather that they should be able to build, and respond to, idea in sound. The 'ideal' of such a process is to be found in the composer rather than in the instrumentalist.

One of the great impediments to curriculum development in music is the strength of the music teacher's training. It enables him to wear new developments on the old framework and to survive, even to embrace, changes in techniques and ideas without altering his basic stance one iota. Here and there one senses a stirring, a real change, on the part of a few brave teachers who can throw the more stifling constraints to the winds and close the window before they blow back in again in another guise. These teachers are pointing in a different direction. They are looking at music as though it never existed before, as though it is something that is made by children. They are looking at children, at the pace, the rhythms, the melodies, the frustrations, the very harmonics of their existence and the idea is taking hold of them that maybe, just maybe, this is what music in schools should be about. These teachers are seeking to develop in the child true medium control which results from reflexive awareness, the awareness of form and idea in process, in the making.

3 Use of realised form

Realised form plays an immense part in the whole structure of music in schools. Since it is the performer or interpreter of established musical works that provides the ideal of music teaching in schools rather than the composer, it is not surprising that pupils are often brought to music as to a shrine. It is there to be played or to be listened to but only the 'Masters' make it. Such a view would be intolerable to an art teacher but then art enters the world at the outset in its 'living' form and music has to be created twice, once by the composer and again by the performer. Since it is the second act

of creation that brings most music teachers into the profession
and not the first it is inevitable that their outlook will differ from
that of the art teacher whose whole training leans towards composition and indeed is unencumbered by any second act of creation.

There are two aspects to the use of realised form. There is the
active production of music in the lesson and in choirs and orchestras, and there is the use of music for appreciation. There is no doubt
that in the establishment of choirs and orchestras many teachers
find their greatest sense of achievement. One cannot help feeling
that it serves as a solace for those who are disillusioned with class
teaching. To be assured of a small band of dedicated musicians
playing impressively at a public performance is the music teacher's
moment of triumph, his hour of vindication.

'We have probably the biggest orchestra in the county. We've
built it up over the last two and a half years. We've some very
good instrumentalists, I suppose about thirty-five or forty; and
when we've performed occasionally in front of the school
people have come up, children have come up and said, "I never
expected to hear anything like that." '

The music teacher can be justly proud of his achievements with
choirs and orchestras and yet they often serve to narrow his sights
to the realisation of the ideal that guided his training and to cause
him to shelve the very real problems of making music an effective
force in the lives of the vast majority of pupils. The teacher quoted
above was justly proud of his thirty-five instrumentalists. No doubt
the remaining one thousand pupils were also proud of them but
nothing that takes place in these concerts will fundamentally alter
the musical participation of the majority although no doubt some
candidates for the orchestra will emerge as a result of the performances having taken place.

If this judgement seems a little harsh it is because the author
believes that the more impressive the achievements of the teachers
in training an élite corps of musicians the more entrenched become
the traditional barriers to widespread participation in musical
experience in the school. When the teacher dreams of orchestras
and choirs he often becomes wistful of some paradise where only
the musical may enter.

'An ideal situation would be a place where I could have a reasonable quantity, and quality, of personnel in choir and orchestra

alike—or choirs and orchestras plural. At the same time the kinds involved would have to do music because they wanted to . . . because they were genuinely interested or because they had a certain amount of ability that they wanted to use, I'd do nothing to force them, nothing at all.'

It is difficult for music teachers to realise that such dreams are often at the root of their problems with class teaching. Many children want to play musical instruments and for a wide variety of different reasons. They may enjoy the sheer accomplishment, the opportunity to perform for others, the ability to play the music they love, etc. If the sole desire of the teacher is to gratify this wish then he may be performing an invaluable service to music and its appreciation in schools but this will not necessarily have anything to do with choirs and orchestras. If the teacher truly seeks to gratify the pupils' needs to play musical instruments then he may find himself in the path of considerable opposition and frustrations as the following account from one such teacher indicates:

'The crux of the problem is my relationship to the music adviser and his department. I stood up in front of the entire school and stated, "What instrument do you want to learn? Come and tell me and I'll arrange it." Over sixty girls came to me. Two girls wanted the accordion, loads wanted the piano and nearly fifty wanted the guitar. Complications over there being no accordions or teachers for it caused that instrument to be abandoned. The piano teacher took half a term in arriving. As for the guitar teacher, it was just the biggest disappointment. All the children are bursting to learn. I held in the end my own guitar classes, awaiting the arrival of the guitar teacher . . . *then [when he arrived] the teacher tells me that out of all those girls dying to learn the guitar he's chosen to teach four.* The rest I'm expected to teach despite the fact that I would prefer to start a recorder class. I stay late to teach choir. I stay late to do a guitar class. I do music and poetry. I'm expected to give singing lessons. They have to be of a certain standard. Loads of forms have to be signed—interviews etc.— all in order to get the one singing teacher—who has to do it?—I have to do it! I can't fit all these children in who want to learn the guitar without giving up more of my lunch hour or after school time to start another two classes. What I feel resentful about is this music adviser who says no to my suggestion that the children should be allowed to learn folk or whatever as long as they're learning to play an instrument. He advises that they learn notes and formal exercises. I feel he can just stick it! just stick it!—that's the biggest drawback, that's what grates. *There's a man who wants an elitist society of musicians and what about the majority—just let 'em go!—How can you let them go when they're burning to play?*'

This is the crux of the problem. Had this teacher set out to create an orchestra and a choir in the traditional sense then no doubt a great deal more assistance and encouragement might have been proffered. Instead the aim was to help the children to master the instruments that they wanted to master in order to play the music that they wanted to play and that was quite another matter. The faces of many music educators are turned against such an idea although few would care to admit it.

Choirs and orchestras can often be an immense and positive force for musical education in the school if they are truly broadly based but they are no substitute for creative music making and performance built from the class work outwards to the school concert. If creative music were the very pivot of music in the school then the existence of choirs and orchestras would cease to threaten the musical education of the majority as they so often do at present.

The part played by musical appreciation, listening to music as distinct from the actual playing of musical works, is very great indeed. Most music teachers incorporate some element of musical appreciation into their lessons and some lean very heavily indeed on the gramophone record. Children will often listen very attentively to music that is played to them and, at the time at least, may find the experience enjoyable and worthwhile. Nevertheless, music for appreciation is rarely integrated with the creative work of the pupil of which there is usually very little in the music lesson, and it frequently exists as an isolated entity on its own. The child's considered judgement of the exercise is consequently much harsher. Children find it difficult to justify the activity of appreciating music in school or to conceive that it can be of educational value. Sheer prejudice does help to reinforce this viewpoint but quite often it is the negative ambience of the music lesson itself which can overcome any immediate gratification gained by the child by causing him to define the situation in indifferent or even hostile terms. Music does have an immediate appeal, however, and music teachers

know that in just getting pupils to listen they take them quite a long way to musical involvement. Their own training supports this idea very strongly. If someone really likes or is moved by a piece of music then his urge to participate, even to play music, is likely to be strengthened.

Encouraging musical appreciation is in itself a very laudable aim and at first glance, it might appear that music teachers show a great deal of open-minded liberality in the matter of what is to be appreciated. Indeed from our interviews with music teachers one would have to conclude that their tastes are very catholic indeed, or rather that their tolerance of the children's tastes is. The right of the children to like all kinds of music is fully recognised and teachers will often devote a great deal of lesson time to indulging pupils tastes rather than their own. One teacher ran what was tantamount to a 'juke-box jury' for one class as a regular event. Pop records were solemnly played, and voting and discussion took place. As the teacher put it to us:

'I don't care what sort of musical appreciation it is. I don't just stick to symphony orchestras. I use folk music, I use jazz, I use pop. Why not? It's music, it's there.'

Why not indeed? And yet a closer look at the music teacher's use of pop music reveals some features which might help to explain why the playing of the pupil's music has not brought all the dividends that the music teacher might have expected it to bring. Despite the immediate appeal that listening to pop records and talking about them has for the pupils, their general response to the music lesson is not, in many cases, improved in the slightest. The truth is that the music teacher is often as pure in heart as a colonial missionary seeking to render the gospel to the natives in their own vernacular. The natives answer him in vernacular, they 'dig the tune' but they 'don't like the backing'. One does not usually have to look very far beneath the surface of the music teacher's use of the 'Cream', 'Led Zeppelin' or the 'Grateful Dead' to find the real package. It comes in the form of 'unusual rhythmic sequences', 'really clever chord progressions' and 'complex harmonies'. Pop music is good because it actually has some clever music in it. So the notion goes with many a 'with it' music teacher. To the pupil this can often seem patronising and strangely irrelevant because it ignores or misconstrues the use that he actually has for pop music.

That pop is 'bait' for catching fish is indicated by many of the statements made to us by music teachers on this subject. The teacher quoted above for example concluded by saying:

'Kids happen to be overflooded with pop music, not that there's anything wrong with it, at least some of it, I try to make the kids aware that there is so much more to music than this, there's centuries of it in the past.'

Another teacher put the issue more forcefully:

'I discussed it with the head and I said, "Really, if I say no you cannot have your pop listening then we'll have a revolution on our hands and I think I must try and meet it half way." *They continue to have their pop music and I do my appreciation.* We divided it and gradually it worked itself out so that I was quite surprised at the end of the third year when not one pop record was chosen, only the classical records came out and they thoroughly enjoyed listening to them.'

Whether the playing of more pop music in schools is particularly relevant to this conversion to classical music is a matter for debate. Pop music is used by pupils as part of a world of experience which does not usually involve music teachers, music lessons or the usual ambience of the school. The music teacher seeks quite different things from the music than the pupil and the more he discusses the musical merits of pop the more he is asking the pupil to put the music to quite a different use and one that is antithetical to the immediate gratification that it affords him. Pop music is not independent of the situations, moods, private and public places, and encounters that characterise adolescent life. Pop music is important to the adolescent inasmuch as it is expressive of part of his cultural milieu and of his consciousness within it. Since in much of school life and certainly in the music lesson the adolescent finds the expression of that consciousness denied, pop music played in schools for appreciation can seem like an empty gesture. It is as though the music teacher is saying, 'I am a non-believer but I promise to visit your church regularly and pray with you provided you never mention the name of your God.'

No doubt there are many examples up and down the country of teachers using pop, folk or jazz for appreciation, for listening to, in an effective manner. It must be said, however, that we observed virtually none of it. In one school only did we observe the appreciation of music tied in to some extent with making music. In most of the others the teacher's use of music for appreciation was not guided by any real understanding of what meaning musical experience has or even could have within the consciousness of the pupils.

4 Personal development

On the whole music teachers had less to say about the personal development of the pupil than any other group of teachers we interviewed. What was particularly striking was the fact that although they were often very aware of developmental changes that affected the pupils' responses to music, their structuring of the curriculum took virtually no notice of these nor was there any evidence of a really serious attempt to deal with the difficulties which these changes presented. What teachers of music noticed about adolescent development in relation to their subject reinforced the basic picture provided in more elaborate form by teachers of the other arts.

'When they first come their responses are very spontaneous. You play them a piece and they light up and away they go. Towards the end of the first year they become very much more conscious of their responses and it's a little bit more restricted, and not quite so spontaneous. It gets worse—they seem to get very self-conscious—and this thing about "I can't sing I haven't got a nice voice, I can't do that, I don't know about music"; and whereas before they would be willing to try anything now we're faced with the problem of low ability plus the restrictions of self-consciousness. Those are the problems that really concern me.'

The art teacher and the drama teacher encounter this same problem of the mid-adolescent's concern about the validity of his expressive act. In drama the teacher is often careful to incorporate material in the curriculum which is relevant to the problems of social adjustment being faced by the pupil. Much of this work is flagrantly 'objective' in orientation, and I have criticised it for that reason but it is at least some kind of attempt to deal with the personal development of the pupil in some relevant sense and it is recognised by most pupils as such. Similarly the expressive movement in art which lays so much emphasis on abstraction is also an attempt to face the personal development problems posed by the mid-adolescent.

The music teacher, on the other hand, makes no such response to these problems. Instead, many music teachers perceive in the adolescent's development only the growing possibility for grasping music intellectually and academically, in the way that a physics teacher might perceive their growing analytical capabilities. The idea is that as soon as the adolescent can actually think and analyse then you can explain to him how music is structured; you can teach him something of its grammar.

'I can talk about things like the science of music, the construction of music to older children. I can talk about the way the chords are produced and constructed—the way harmony is constructed —the way melodic phrases are created; but to a twelve-year-old this would be Chinese. It's just that at the age of twelve you've got to say, "Right, here's the song, here's the tune." You let the child sing it and play it whatever it happens to be. But if the child uses his ears and I play a wrong chord he will say, "That's wrong!" "Why is it wrong?" "Sounds funny!" So you correct it. You don't explain why it's wrong, you just correct it.'

Following this response I questioned this teacher rather closely about what he thought were the differences in the actual experience of music as between older and younger pupils. The only answer was the disclosure that the youngest children liked music with a story to it. Experience with questioning other music teachers and one music adviser on this point drew the same rather frustrating innocently deceptive blank. It was always as though the music teachers were denying that the question could have any meaning in relation to music. They were not denying that people made some music for younger children and some for older. What they appeared to be denying was that this distinction had any real meaning in purely musical terms, whatever social or cultural connotations it might have. This was put to us quite clearly by the music teacher from the school with the highest (indeed the most overwhelming) response to music of any of the schools that we researched.

'If I were to give the older girls a song, with say nursery rhyme words they would "pooh pooh" it although the actual tune was very nice. I was talking to the girls about it yesterday. I said, "It's really rather ridiculous because if you think about it we have Top of the Pops in the lunch hour when the first years come to listen to it as well as the fifth years and no-one says— this is babyish, the first years are here! With one first year group I did two nursery rhymes put together, 'Hickory Dickory Dock' and 'Three Blind Mice' and at first even the eleven-year-olds thought this was a bit much—but of course when they realised that it wasn't quite as easy as they thought then they put their teeth into it and thoroughly enjoyed it; and in the process of this happening fourth-year girls came in and said, 'Gosh, isn't it good, can we have a go?' Whereas If I'd tried to include them from the outset they would have said, 'You're joking, you must be off your rocker.'''

To understand why the teacher of music regards social and cultural divisions concerning music for different ages as having little 'musical' foundation one has to remember the enormous use made in music of the realised form, the set piece. The children are more usually involved in the enactment of someone else's musical idea and not in the creation of their own musical idea. Their own experience in response to the idea is not apparent in the enactment. Realised forms of most kinds can be used by adolescents and children at different ages for quite different reasons. In the incident described above it was very possible that the first-year girls had a quite different experience from the fourth-year girls though they both enjoyed it equally. The music teacher is therefore right, at least in the sense that realised form will often span the age range with each age group responding in its own way. As a rule the music teacher regards the nature of the response to realised form as a private and individual affair. He is concerned to know that there has been a positive response, not what the nature of that response is.

The problem with this attitude is that it involves the teacher in a hit-and-miss affair with the consciousness of the developing adolescent. Certainly it ensures that music plays no consistent part in the child's development. What kind of experience is relevant at different ages, and the musical possibilities for realising the child's development are hardly ever thought about.

The more the teaching of music is inspired by the ideal of creative music-making, however, the more the teacher of music will discover about the ways in which children actually use musical experience at different stages in their development. This knowledge is vital if music teachers are to build curricula that the pupils will find relevant. The barest inkling of such knowledge is worth all of the crotchet-to-apple transformations that there ever could be.

5 Examinations and assessment

Examinations are very much an entrenched part of the academic music scene. Since most of the pupils who go on to do music after the third year are usually those with instrumental proficiency, academic interest or both, the formal examination seems to many teachers to be ideal for assessing progress. They quarrel with it no more than would the mathematics teacher. What these teachers are seeking to assess is a response that is every bit as right or wrong as a response to the mathematics lesson. 'If you know your music, then the answers will be right; if you do not know your music they will be wrong. If you play your instrument proficiently the expert will grade you accordingly.' The following is a summary description of the type of lesson that leads up to this kind of examination.

'The lesson lasted for two hours, and covered a wide range of activities in turn. After a singing practice for a carol service, the group turned to course work with an exercise on non-essential note analysis, carried through in a businesslike, almost mathematical way. There followed a study of the opening theme of the Bach Brandenburg Concerto No. 1 and then the teacher dictated some notes on concerti grossi in general and the six Brandenburg Concerti in particular. The lesson finished with an exercise in which the pupils had to write down a tune played on the piano. The pupils had little chance to engage their own experience or their own feelings. In fact it appeared to be the teacher's explicit aim to replace any personal subjective judgement of the pupil by an objective, almost mathematical appraisal. The entire atmosphere was indistinguishable from that prevailing in a sixth-year physics group.'

One can only commiserate with the composer Martinu who, on failing his music examinations, commented:

'I cannot learn anything, I must come to it through feeling.'

Indeed, whenever a music teacher does approach music from the perspective of the creative music-maker he or she experiences the same frustrations with respect to formal academic examinations as the teachers of the other arts. Again C.S.E. appears to these teachers as something of a knight to the rescue:

> 'This thing about exams which is so much a part of our society —having to obtain certificates for this and that. The movement teacher and I have made a combined syllabus. I don't know whether it's going to be accepted or not . . . my emphasis has been upon performance and the use of music rather than doing marvellous harmony papers, sitting down and doing fantastic oral tests and history papers—that's out. I've justified it by saying we are all coming to the performance. The history will come into it in the projects that they do—and the rest of it—the rudiments of music—will be in their own compositions, which they can perform or get others to perform. It is their awareness and use of music when they start off—the minute that they come into the school—that will really be put to the test when they produce perhaps their own dance drama, painting to music, light shows, something within their experience and within their environment. And this is what I am trying to combat in my syllabus—the formal structure of a so-called exam.'

Curriculum structure

The strongly academic training of music teachers usually encourages them to structure their curricula quite considerably, more especially when they are working within an examination framework. Even when they are not, however, there is a tendency to establish a structure in respect of the order in which certain things are taught, e.g. melody, harmony, etc., in a way that is strongly influenced by the teacher's own formal training. Invariably it is the technical aspects of music-making that determine the structure unless teachers are explicitly trying to break away into the field of creative music-making. Then they are inclined, as is the teacher quoted above, to structure in accordance with the pupils' interests and needs in a way that is relevant to their personal development. The internal structuring of the music lesson was invariably very strong whatever the basis. Music teachers approach their work tidily at least. Many of them have a keenly developed sense of order.

Curriculum content

With one notable exception music teachers observed by us showed little adventurous or imaginative spirit in their selection of material. They would appear to be embarrassed by riches if one were to judge of their modest 'presentations' selected from the vast wealth of their musical heritage. On the whole the music teachers we spoke to seemed to select their music under two labels 'the kind of serious music I find interesting' and 'pop' which the pupils like and which the teacher might like as well. What emerges then is a sort of potpourri which samples the world of music in a way that is thoroughly unrepresentative. Music covers a vast range of human experience and is used in myriad ways to develop that experience. Music teachers do not often explore this range simply because they do not pay sufficient attention in their work to the experience itself, as distinct from the technical aspects of music-making.

Mode of encounter

The principal mode of encounter in the music lesson is a combination of the conducted choir practice and formal academic class teaching. The former is used in connection with performance and the latter when academic or analytical music teaching is taking place. In music appreciation sessions there is naturally a period of discussion which is usually similar to the kind of discussion that takes place in an English lesson in relation to a text.

Communication networks

The usual network involves a decidedly asymmetrical channel between the teacher and the pupils. He addresses them as a class or as individuals within the class. They respond to his commands or answer his questions. When there is a discussion the children's views are usually channelled through him. Formal group networks were rarely set up by the teachers we observed nor was there much work with individuals except in the case of the teacher quoted earlier who favoured a strongly creative music-making approach. This teacher used all types of communication network depending on the outcome of the work. As far as the actual dimensions of the channels are concerned, and their capacity to carry broad or narrow bands of messages, the music lessons we observed showed considerable variation. Where the pupil's endorsement of the lesson was highest it was noted that communication channels were broadest. There was a warm and relaxed atmosphere and a fairly free flow of information between teacher and pupils and, when required, among pupils themselves.

7   The Pupils

So far we have probed a little way into the consciousness of arts teachers in respect of the curriculum but, what about the pupils? The pupil's definition of the situation, his consciousness of the educational encounter, is vital to the effectiveness of any curriculum. Insufficient attention has been paid in educational research to the pupil's choices and evaluations regarding curricula. It is often assumed that the teacher's personality and his style of teaching assure him of a positive or negative response as the case may be. These things are undoubtedly of great importance but the matter is by no means as straightforward as that. The truth is that there are powerful forces quite outside them which can sometimes overshadow any or all of them in the shaping of the pupil's response, and very often great differences in the apparent competences of two teachers reveal the minutest differences in the 'shape' and quantity of pupil evaluations and choices in respect of their curricula. The importance of this fact can hardly be underestimated because a fundamental assumption of curriculum development is that the mode of engagement with curriculum is improved by the innovations introduced. This may or may not be so but it is certainly assumed and therefore the factors that determine the general orientation of the pupils, their definitions of the situation, are of critical importance to the curriculum developer. The problem is that so little is at present known about these factors, but that is all the more reason for starting to look. There is no point in dismissing the pupil's response as irrational or immature, or in blinding oneself to the fact that his definition of the situation seriously affects the entire outcome of the educational encounter. Such an attitude is ultimately self-defeating. As the American sociologist W. I. Thomas once put it, 'If a man defines his situation to be real then it is real in its consequences'.

A very good indication of the importance that pupils attach to different subjects within the curriculum can be found in the pupil's stated preferences with respect to the subjects themselves. There have been attempts to elicit information of this kind, and the interested reader is referred to the Schools Council's *Enquiry One*[1] for a recent and quite comprehensive attempt to do this in the case of school-leaving classes. A somewhat different procedure was adopted in the present study, however. The pupils were not asked to state their preferences as such but to construct their own (hypothetical) curriculum from a list of some twenty different subjects for the 'next ten school periods'. They were allowed to devote up to five school periods to any one subject but no more. They were thus able to make up a ten-period curriculum consisting of as few as two subjects (if they devoted as many as five periods to each) or as many as ten subjects (if they devoted as little as one period to each). As one might expect, most pupils opted for something between the two extremes. The point about this exercise is that the pupils are engaged in the economic game of 'marginal utility'. Every extra school period they devote to art for example will cost them some other period that they cannot have, say a second period of maths. They must engage in a balancing exercise which is not too different from the task facing those responsible for constructing the time-table. Since the cost of lessons chosen must be weighed in terms of lessons foregone it seems probable that the pupil's responses provide a more reliable indication of the true weight of his choices relative to one another than any exercise which involved him in merely listing subjects in order of preference.

There were some five thousand pupils of all ages in the six secondary schools involved. The chart below (Fig. 1, p. 141) gives the overall structure of the pupils' choices within the curriculum for all six schools taken together. In this and the subsequent analyses the sixth year has been omitted thereby reducing the sample to 3,882 pupils. As the sixth year is not entirely comparable with the other five, we thought it best to omit it although in point of fact including it would not have changed the picture significantly.

As we travel down the chart we move from the least chosen subjects to the most chosen subjects. It will be noted that the least chosen subject is music. An average of 78% of the pupils do not devote even one of their ten school periods to it whereas for Drama, Art, and English the percentage goes down to 60½%, 57%, and

[1] *Enquiry One—Young School Leavers*, H.M.S.O., 1968.

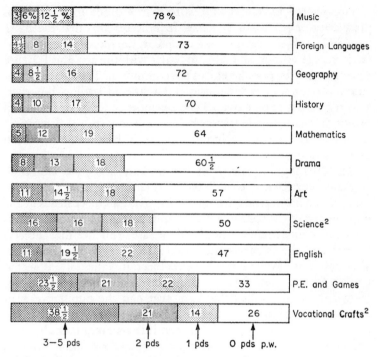

| | | 78 % | Music |
| 3½% | 12½ % | | |

(chart)

1. Pupils constructed a hypothetical curriculum for the 'next ten school periods'

2. As explained on p. 119, science and vocational crafts are 'artifacts', and the figures must be treated with caution

FIG. 1 PUPILS' CURRICULUM CHOICE—Percentage who allocated 0 periods, 1 period, etc. to each subject[1] (N = 3,882 pupils)

47% respectively. The highest number of choices of all go to the vocational craft subjects. For certain computational reasons[1] the choices for science and vocational crafts may be somewhat inflated in relation to the other subjects. Nevertheless there is good reason to believe that the distortion is not very great. These are in any case very frequently chosen subjects even when we allow for this bias.

[1] There were a number of subjects listed that the pupils could choose within the general categories of science and vocational crafts. This meant that there was a greater probability that one of these would be chosen. Other subjects such as English or Mathematics offered only one opportunity for selection.

This overall look gives us more than a guide to the general popularity of particular subjects. It indicates also that the more 'academic' subjects tend to be unpopular, the more 'participatory' subjects, the vocational crafts, together with the arts and P.E. are established at the popular end of the continuum. The two apparent exceptions are science and music. It is a little misleading, however, to consider the pupil's overall choices independently of the actual provision that is made for them. Fig. 2 below (p. 143) compares the pupils' overall curriculum choices with the average provision in their schools.

The dividing line between the broadly academic and non-academic curricula is established at drama. The two exceptions can now be more easily accounted for. Although science is at the popular end of the continuum the pupils want almost a quarter less than is provided in their schools. In the case of all the other subjects at that end the pupils want more than is provided. Similarly, although music is the least chosen subject, it is the only subject at the 'unpopular' end of which the pupils do not choose less than is provided. In all other subjects at that end the pupils do want less than is provided. Thus if we interpret popularity in terms of the excess of choice over provision then it is apparent that all of the academic subjects including science are under-chosen in relation to provision, and the non-academic subjects are over-chosen in relation to provision, with the exception of music where choice matches provision.

We need, however, to put this in some kind of perspective as far as different age groups are concerned. Art, drama, and music are usually compulsory subjects during the first three years but optional after that. By and large this was the case in our schools as well, although the type of option system varied considerably from school to school as one might expect. The provision for English however remains constant throughout. What differences can we discern in the pupil's construction of a curriculum as between the different years? Fig. 3 below (p. 144) gives the pupils' curriculum choices year by year for each subject from the first year through to the fifth year.

On the whole the pupils' choices remain remarkably consistent over time. If a subject has a low endorsement relative to provision as does mathematics then it tends to maintain this in all five years. The same is true if it has a high endorsement relative to provision

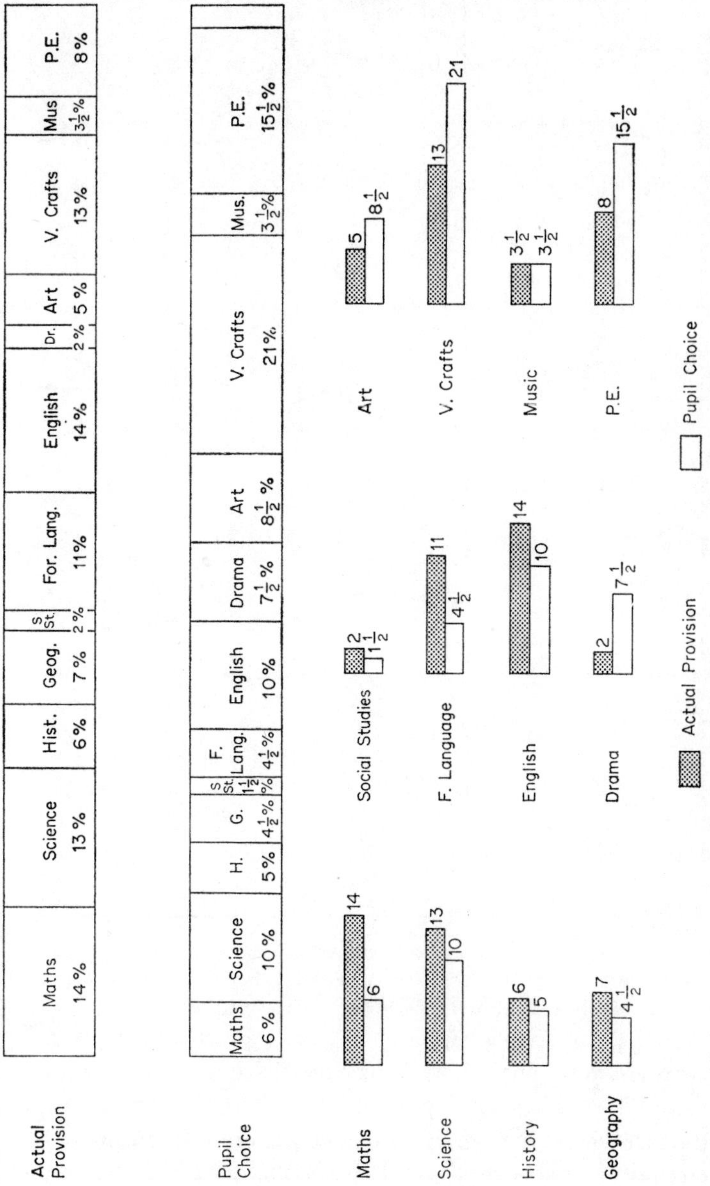

Actual Provision	Maths 14%	Science 13%	Hist. 6%	Geog. 7%	S. St. 2%	For. Lang. 11%	English 14%	Dr. 2%	Art 5%	V. Crafts 13%	Mus 3½%	P.E. 8%

Pupil Choice	Maths 6%	Science 10%	H. 5%	G. 4½%	S.St. 1½%	F. Lang. 4½%	English 10%	Drama 7½%	Art 8½%	V. Crafts 21%	Mus. 3½%	P.E. 15½%

FIG. 2   THE CURRICULUM—A comparison of actual provision and pupil choice in six research schools: 1st to 5th years

Maths — 14 / 6

Science — 13 / 10

History — 6 / 5

Geography — 7 / 4½

Social Studies — 2 / 1½

F. Language — 11 / 4½

English — 14 / 10

Drama — 2 / 7½

Art — 5 / 8½

V. Crafts — 13 / 21

Music — 3½ / 3½

P.E. — 8 / 15½

■ Actual Provision   □ Pupil Choice

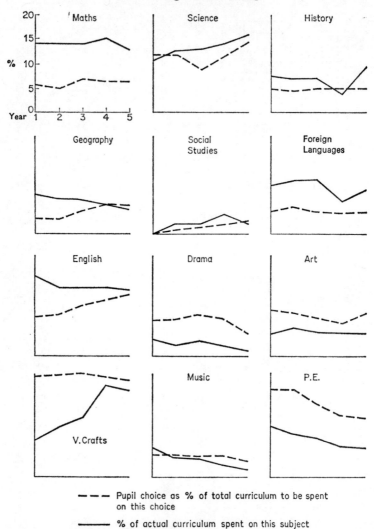

FIG. 3 SUBJECTS AS PERCENTAGE OF CURRICULUM—
Actual provision and pupil choice in six research schools, 1st to 5th years

as is the case with P.E. or drama. Pupil choice does not appear to be related in any simple way to actual provision. Sometimes it appears to take no account of it at all, as in the case of vocational crafts. Sometimes it moves with changes in provision, as in the case of P.E.

and science, and sometimes it moves despite provision as in the case of geography and English, both of which improve steadily in our schools. It is important to remind the reader that these data apply only to our six schools. They are most certainly not generalisable with any statistical justification for schools beyond these. As far as our six schools are concerned, however, the pupils' choices in building their own curriculum show a remarkable consistency over time in the face of quite strong academic pressures. There appears to be a definite logic in the pupil's choices which should tell us something of their definition of the situation so far as curriculum is concerned, if we can articulate it.

Of course it may be argued that the pupils choose irresponsibly, endorsing all the 'glamour' subjects and failing to maintain a sense of overall balance which those responsible for the time-table must provide. If this is the case then the pupils reveal a remarkable consistency in doing this not only at all ages but in all types of school and over all intelligence ranges. In any case such a view merely begs the question and makes the assumption that 'academic' subjects are naturally not interesting or exciting for children. Those dedicated to curriculum development in sciences, mathematics and the humanities are unlikely to agree with that point of view.

It is possible to perceive a very simple logic in the pupils' choice behaviour. The non-academic curriculum accounts for some 32% of actual provision in their schools. They have raised this to 56%. They have reduced the 68% of academic provision to 41½%. The major 'casualties' of their curriculum are mathematics and foreign languages and to a lesser extent science and English. The major beneficiaries are vocational crafts, P.E. and drama, and to a lesser extent art.

What the pupils appear to be reflecting in their choices is a demand for a curriculum that involves them personally to a much greater extent. On the whole they have endorsed those areas of the curriculum that involve them personally, physically, and creatively on the one hand, and those that are directly related to practical or vocational skills on the other. The children place very great value indeed on subjects which give them an opportunity to live out something of themselves, to make statements that include them and to feel that something they do is vital to the outcome. When we come to our two academic grammar schools it is apparent that the demand for these participatory subjects is, if anything, greater in

TABLE 1 THE CURRICULUM—Pupil curriculum choice and actual curriculum provision in six research schools (1st to 5th years)

	Sec. Modern				Grammar				Comprehensive				All six research schools	
	School A		School B		School C		School D		School E		School F			
	P	A	P	A	P	A	P	A	P	A	P	A	P	A
	%	%	%	%	%	%	%	%	%	%	%	%	%	%
Maths	7	14	5½	15	6	15	4½	13	5	16	7	14	6	14
Science	8½	7	11	8	11	15	16½	15	10	14	9½	16	10	13
History	3½	*	4½	9	4½	6	6	6	8	5	3½	5	5	6
Geography	1½	*	3½	10	5	6	4	6	7	6	4½	6	4½	7
Social Studies	2½	*	1	—	1½	1	2½	1	2	2	½	2	1½	2
Foreign Languages	4½	3	3	9	5½	17	7	17	4	10½	4	8	4½	11
English	12½	12	9	17	7½	15	8½	13	8½	16	11½	14	10	14
Drama (+ Dance)	5½	3	7	—	5	1	7½	2	4½	2	10	3	7½	2
Art	8	*	11	4	11	4	8	6	10½	5	6½	5	8½	5
Vocational Crafts	25½	19	18	15	19½	8	16½	6½	21	13	23	17	21	13
Music	4½	*	11	6	3	4	2½	4	2	2	3	2	3½	3½
P.E.	13½	6	14	8	20	8	14	10	17	9	15	7	15½	8
*I.D.E.		*37												

[P = Pupil curriculum choice; A = Actual curriculum provision]

Note 1 These figures apply to the six research schools only. Our sample has more grammar school pupils and fewer secondary modern school pupils than would occur in a national sample, and therefore the data is not representative of *all* pupils and schools, and should not be used for extrapolation.

Note 2 In each school there is a miscellaneous category in the actual curriculum, which has been ignored here (i.e. R.I., Careers, Library, Counselling, Visits, etc.) On average, the twelve subjects listed above occupy 93% of the total curriculum of the six research schools.

Note 3 Science = physics, chemistry, biology, and general science.

Vocational crafts = woodwork, metalwork, technical drawing, shorthand/typing, needlework, domestic science, home economics, etc.

For certain computational reasons, the pupil choice figures for 'science' and 'vocational' crafts may be slightly inflated and must be treated with caution (see p. 141).

relation to provision than in the less academic environments of our secondary modern and comprehensive schools. The table opposite (p. 146) compares the pupil demand with the actual provision for each subject in each of our six schools.

While it is undoubtedly true that if left to their own devices the pupils would increase the emphasis placed upon practical, physical and creative activities at the expense of the academic ones it is most certainly not true that they can necessarily accept all curricula that give them the opportunity to be creative, or to participate actively. In both their interviews with us and their questionnaire responses the pupils manifest two somewhat contradictory orientations. They appear to want the opportunity to move out, to express their individuality, to participate. They also want to feel safe, to have clear guidelines and parameters to work within, to be sure of the floor beneath them, the walls around them and the way ahead. The pupil's need for security can thus conflict with his need to express himself. A need for security is natural of course but the active process of successful negotiation of the environment leading to discovery can in itself bring this sense of security to the individual more effectively than anything else. Our problem is that formal education, from the very beginning, tends to divorce the requirement for security from the need for active participation and self-expression. It encourages a neurotic involvement with security because the ability of the child to do anything or to move out in any direction is tied up very strongly with the notion that there are pre-existent rules that must be followed *before* engagement with the world can take place. The child often does not discover these in active practice but learns them by precept and rote. Education becomes a breeding ground for self-fulfilling prophecies because the child comes to start with the rule or technique and then discover its effectiveness in achieving a particular result. It is little wonder that many children will not move at all unless they are given instructions on how to do so first. The strong academic orientation of our educational system enhances this rule-directed approach to life and with it a consciousness within pupils that reduces their whole sense of security to the act of grasping the rules and sticking to them. School is the place where a corpus of knowledge and techniques is imparted. There is an almost universal acceptance on the part of our young that these are somehow indispensable to proper functioning always assuming that you want to function at all in a given area. The pupils find it far easier to choose not to function in an area (e.g. to reject academic subjects) than to accept that they can operate without the rule-directed academic framework in the areas that they do select for functioning. When the child says 'No' to the academic curricula he does not also say 'No' to the academic *modus operandi*. He is still the victim of the need for preconceptions and techniques upon which his sense of security has become dependent for reassurance.

The adolescent therefore finds himself in the contradictory position of wanting to take an active, participatory and creative rôle, to make discoveries and to innovate, and yet at the same time of wanting to know where he's going, what steps he should take, what the end result will be and how valid is the whole thing in terms of criteria external to the activity. He wants to be free to express himself and rule-directed at one and the same time. Self-expression always proceeds with constraints, but when it is truly creative the most important of these are discovered reflexively as the idea is made in the medium even where formal techniques and preconceptions have been employed from the outset. It is the 'outset' that has become so important to our adolescents. Their spirits cry out against an academic system that has done much to remove them from any personal involvement with their own activity and has denied them the right to exercise and express themselves in the process of their development in school; and yet in order to control the process of self-expression (and thereby feel reasonably secure) they demand that when they are given the opportunity to express themselves there should be a strong enough framework of prescriptions and techniques to assure them how to proceed, what to expect at the end and how to evaluate the outcome. Because they are so used to operating from this prescriptive rule-directed base, they give themselves little opportunity to exercise and develop the reflexive control that was discussed earlier. The adolescent is thus caught in a trap which the most dedicated advocates of free expression find the greatest difficulty in unlocking.

We saw that the arts teachers are often halfway between the rule-directed control of the medium and reflexive control of the medium. Having forsaken the one they have not yet achieved the other. The pupil strongly rejects this halfway house. Without being able to establish reflexive control (or in most cases even being aware of what it is) he is loth to attempt to function without rule-direction. When a teacher committed to the ideology of personal development through creative discovery attempts to free the pupil and encourage him to express himself he may meet with the most disheartening rejection unless he is also able to develop sufficient reflexive control of the medium in the pupil to permit the latter a real opportunity to develop. The crux of the matter is this. Control of the medium is essential to all development and all expression. If development is to take place at all then there must be control of the medium. If this is not reflexive then it will be rule-directed. The 'enlightened' teacher who fails to recognise this is offering the child a freedom that is no better than the freedom to learn nothing. He must not then be surprised if the pupil rejects this freedom, forsaking it for the technique-ridden traditions that the teacher may despise. The pupil cannot use freedom effectively unless reflexive control of the medium is within his competence.

I have already argued this case for the teachers but what evidence can be adduced from the responses of the pupils in our investigation? Perhaps the first thing that we might note is that within the curriculum the greatest opportunity to participate actively, creatively and expressively within a strong rule-directed framework, with clear guidelines as to procedure and with outcomes that can be objectively evaluated, is provided by the vocational crafts. Physical Education and games also demand this active individual participation and commitment within a strong rule-directed framework and, as we have seen already, it is vocational crafts followed by P.E. and games that lead the pupils' chosen curriculum accounting together for an average of $36\frac{1}{2}\%$ of their total curriculum as compared with the 21% average provision in their schools.

Some of the most interesting clues to the pupils' definition of the situation emerge from comparisons between two schools that have been matched for type and also ability and socio-economic background of the pupils. Where the styles of the teachers can be contrasted the choices of the pupils and their evaluation of lessons produce quite startling divergencies. Let us take the case of music. Music is on the whole rejected by the majority of pupils in secondary schools and is in any case poorly provided for within the curriculum. The pupils' evaluations reveal it to be in a very poor position in relation to art or drama. It is not that they regard it as an academic subject but rather as one which, in their terms, is a failed art subject. They feel on the whole that it encourages participation and self-expression strictly on its own terms and of a kind which does not engage them.

There were of course notable exceptions, and we must now look at two of these. They involve two music departments in 'matched' schools. Both departments are relatively successful in somewhat different respects. They received the highest endorsement from pupils of any of our schools[1] and yet they represent extremely divergent approaches to music teaching. Both departments offer the pupils the opportunity to participate actively and to express themselves but under different conditions. In the case of department A, the approach of the teaching might be described as modern, free, creative. The pupils are encouraged to express themselves in their own individual ways, whether in writing protest songs or whatever and the barest minima of constraints are employed so far as music-making itself is concerned. The teaching is such as to give them encouragement and advice and conveys a total commitment to the musical expression of the pupils. The teaching is decidedly non-academic in style although it is not what some people might term 'way out'. In the case of department B, on the other hand, the children receive a lot of clear direction and prescription as to how they are to go about doing this and that. The music teaching is traditional in style, giving a great deal of opportunity to the pupils to sing away for all they are worth, and to those who can play musical instruments the chance to add their bit. The whole atmosphere is one of warm and enthusiastic participation. The teacher has strong ideas about music and she certainly does not lose any opportunity to make these known to the pupils, but she is completely tolerant of their right to their tastes and very warm towards them. They can have their say and listen to their pop music on occasion but they listen when she has her say and plays them her kind of music. The pupils are mostly engaged in responding to sets of very clear instructions but successful and lusty participation is within their grasp, at least in terms of singing. They are kept on the go all the time. Music is a 'homework' subject and is taken very seriously indeed. If one can sum up the differences between the two approaches one would say that in the case of department A the pupils

---

[1] The fact that the pupils were girls in secondary modern schools accounted for some of this higher level of endorsement, but in all probability not for very much of it.

are being told, 'Here is a chance to be yourself, to express yourself, to beat the drum or write the song or whatever. Here is a chance to be creative. Your ideas really matter. Technique will come later. You'll develop it when you need it.' In the case of department B they are being told, 'Here is your chance to participate actively and get a lot of fun out of making something worthwhile. This is a serious business and we can get fantastic results if you proceed exactly as I tell you. Here's where we're going and you'll know how much we've all achieved when we put on the performance.' I hope that the teachers concerned will forgive me for caricaturing their styles somewhat, but this was necessary to emphasise the contrast that I have in mind.

The teachers in both cases are extremely popular with their pupils. They provide examples of participatory music-making with and without emphasis on control of the medium. Department A illustrates some of the best spirit of the modern 'creative' music teachers in schools who, in the opinion of the author, have relinquished rule-direction without yet having developed methods of instituting reflexive control of the medium. Department B on the other hand illustrates the best of the traditional approach which embraces rule-directed control of the medium but uses it to make active participation on the part of the pupil as full and effective as possible. It must be noted however that department A was not 'soft', expecting nothing from the pupils, nor was department B seeking to create an élite corps of musicians. Having said all this we can now compare the curriculum choices with respect to music relative to the other subjects in these two schools.

It is apparent from the pupils' curriculum that department B with its rule-directed participatory approach has succeeded in achieving a higher level of endorsement than is reflected in any of the schools that we researched. Indeed it has succeeded in raising music from the bottom choice to the third from the top in the pupils' curriculum, following only vocational crafts and P.E. This in itself is quite an astonishing fact and is indicative of the possibilities for engendering a positive attitude towards music on the part of pupils who are not musically literate nor good instrumentalists, in fact pupils who could hardly be more typical of the average and below average. Department A is not unsuccessful either in terms of endorsement by the pupils. Music is raised from the floor to share third place from bottom with foreign languages.

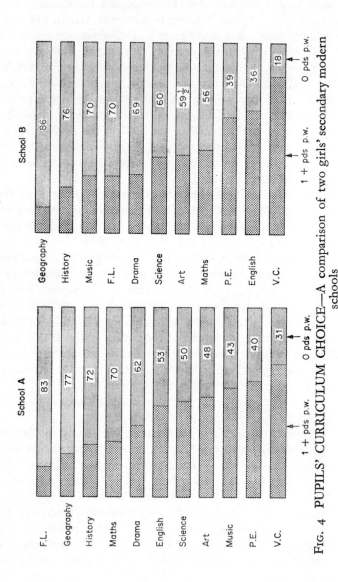

FIG. 4 PUPILS' CURRICULUM CHOICE—A comparison of two girls' secondary modern schools

The Pupils

In all of our other schools music is on the bottom of the pupils' curriculum. Nevertheless, despite the dedication of department A and the 'pupil-centred' creative approach that is used the pupils have not responded with anything like the level of endorsement with which they greet music in department B.

It is possible to explain these results in a number of different ways but naturally the explanation that appeals to the author is the one he has been advancing throughout. Both departments afford some opportunity for active participation. The greater opportunity for creative expression is provided by department A in fact. With department B we can sum up the spirit of participation as a rousing 'let the people sing' appeal. Department A, however, has not developed means of ensuring that the pupils are reflexively in control of the medium as they embark upon a piece of creative work. Rule-direction and formal technique have been largely abandoned on the grounds that they stifle creative involvement and spontaneity of response but they have not been adequately replaced with reflexive control of the medium. When the pupil loses control of the medium in which he is working creatively and cannot regain it then he loses respect for the work that he is doing for the simple reason that self-expression is not possible unless he can institute that control whether in active execution or in appreciation. The pupils are quite simply anxious about the value of what they are doing and if progress really is being made many of them are actually not aware of it. Department B on the other hand relies strongly on rule-directed control of the medium. The pupils are given the opportunity to feel in control as they make music simply because they are left in no doubt about the way to begin, how to proceed and where it is all leading. There is a great atmosphere of warmth and enthusiasm and the pupils seem to know what they are 'making' and how to make it. On the whole there is a great deal less opportunity for individualism and self-expression than is the case in department A but what opportunity there is can actually be utilised fully by the pupils. In department A one suspects that this is not always the case.

We can pursue this notion more fully if we introduce the actual evaluations of their lessons produced for us by the pupils. As part of the questionnaire that they completed the pupils were given ten statements, six of them positive and four negative which they could endorse for each of the lessons in which we were interested, i.e. art, music, drama, and English. We added mathematics and geography as two non-arts subjects that would serve as 'controls'. The pupils were simply invited to endorse only those statements that they felt were true of the particular lesson and if they did not feel that a statement was true of that lesson they need not tick it. The statements were designed to provide a reasonably comprehensive list of evaluative criteria covering such things as novelty and interest, importance, self-expression, clear direction, teacher support, etc. The ten statements were as follows. The six positive statements are listed first and the four negative statements last. When they were actually presented to the pupils they were all interposed together.

1. In my ____ lessons there are lots of new and interesting things to do.
2. In my ____ lessons I feel I have learned something important to me.
3. In my ____ lessons I am allowed to develop my own ideas and do things in my own way.
4. In my ____ lessons I am told clearly what to do and how to do it.
5. My ____ lessons are fun and I really enjoy myself.
6. In my ____ lessons the teacher gives me all the help I need to improve my work.
7. In my ____ lessons there are no new and interesting things to do.
8. In my ____ lessons I feel I haven't learned anything important to me.
9. My ____ lessons are boring and I don't enjoy myself.
10. In my ____ lessons the teacher does not give me enough help to improve my work.

If we compare the pupils' endorsements for the music lesson in the two schools to which I have been referring we get the following picture. (See Fig. 5 opposite.)

There are few differences between the two sets of pupils in their negative endorsements of the lesson. On the whole both sets of pupils are loth to evaluate the lesson negatively, and this reflects the warmth that most of them feel towards their teachers. It is the amount of positive evaluation that each group musters for each statement that reveals something of the situation that exists in the case of the pupils' curriculum choice. Department B's pupils evaluate their music more highly in all positive statements bar one and that is statement 3—'In my music lessons I am encouraged to develop my own ideas and do things in my own way.' When it

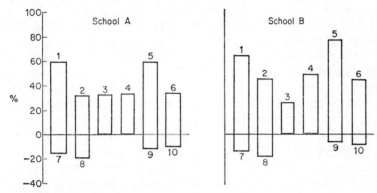

Ten evaluative statements:

1. In my —— lessons there are lots of new and interesting things to do.
2. In my —— lessons I feel I have learned something important to me.
3. In my —— lessons, I am allowed to develop my own ideas and do things in my own way.
4. In my —— lessons I am told clearly what to do and how to do it.
5. My —— lessons are fun and I really enjoy myself.
6. In my —— lessons the teacher gives me all the help I need to improve my work.
7. In my —— lessons there are no new and interesting things to do.
8. In my —— lessons I feel I haven't learned anything important to me.
9. My —— lessons are boring and I don't enjoy myself.
10. In my —— lessons the teacher does not give me enough help to improve my work.

FIG. 5 PUPIL EVALUATION OF *MUSIC* LESSON—Pattern of responses in two girls' secondary modern schools

comes to receiving sufficient help from the teacher to improve their work and being told clearly what to do and taught how to do it, department A's pupils produce a 34% endorsement for both whereas department B's pupils manage 45% and 49% respectively. For novelty and interest department B still has the edge in the pupil's endorsements but not by so much this time (65% to 59%). Pupils of department B find music very much more important

(45% to 31%) and more fun (77% to 60%). The significance of the levels of endorsement achieved is a great deal more apparent when one realises that the levels of endorsement for statement 5—'My music lessons are fun and I really enjoy myself'—ranged from 17% to 38% in all our other schools. Within our sample therefore, both of the departments are highly successful.

The point of making this comparison was not to assert the superiority of rule-direction over free expression. On the contrary I personally believe that the future lies with the relatively less successful (in terms of pupil evaluations) of the two departments. There are greater potentialities for the pupils' personal development in the method of department A but for the pupils to utilise them they require to be able to control the medium reflexively. One might say of the two approaches that in the case of department A a high potential is incompletely realised and in the case of department B a lower potential is completely realised. If the abandoning of rule-directed control by department A leads eventually to satisfactory methods of helping the pupils to achieve reflexive control of the medium then the greater potential of its approach has a chance of being fully realised.

Naturally the definitive statement on a teacher's work is not provided by the pupils' endorsements in an exercise of this kind but these endorsements do reveal a great deal about the organisation of teaching of a given subject in a particular school as we shall see shortly. If we look at the pattern of responses to the ten statements for each subject some very interesting differences become apparent.

If we take the extremes, that is art and maths, there appears to be a definite 'arts shape' for the former and an 'academic shape' for the latter. The high points of the art profile for the six positive statements are statements 1, 3, and 5 which are those dealing with novelty and interest, developing one's own ideas and fun and enjoyment. The low points are statements 2, 4, and 6, dealing with importance, clear direction and teacher support. When we look at the profile for mathematics we find that the exact opposite is the case. Statements 2, 4, and 6 rate high and 1, 3, and 5 rate low. It is also interesting to note that actual negative endorsement is much higher for mathematics than it is for art. The profile for drama, as one might expect is similar to that of art. Geography reveals the same pattern as mathematics but to a much less marked extent and

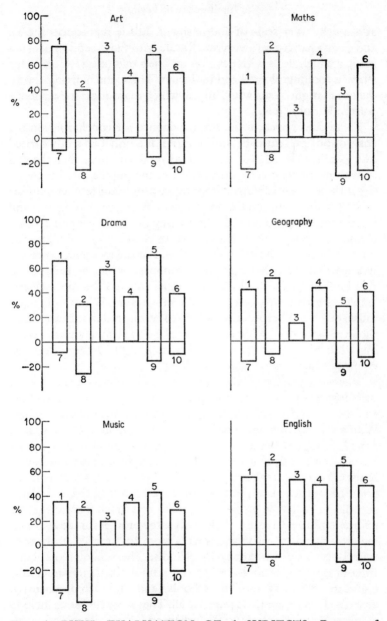

Fig. 6 PUPIL EVALUATION OF 6 SUBJECTS—Pattern of responses to ten statements (see p. 155) for all pupils, in six research schools, 1st–5th years

at a much lower scale of endorsement. Music reproduces the art and drama pattern on a very small scale with the exception of statement 5 which deals with developing one's own ideas. Already the shape is looking blurred and indistinct. This same blurring is produced at a higher level with English which reproduces the academic pattern but only just.

There does appear to be some evidence for concluding on the basis of our present data, and of those of a previous study carried out in thirty-six schools with fourth-year children, that there is something of an inverse correlation in the pupil's mind between the notion that a subject is important, providing teacher support and clear direction, and the notion that it is fun, providing new and interesting things to do and encouraging one to develop one's own ideas. At the present time this inverse correlation is undergoing more rigorous statistical investigation. For the moment, however, it is possible to see that the overall responses of the pupils do reveal this kind of 'shape' and that it is more marked the more clearly 'expressive' or clearly 'academic' the subjects are. With English and music one would expect the pattern to be blurred in this way since the shadow of the academician looms behind so much music teaching while many an 'artistic' soul is struggling to emerge from the confines of academic English teaching.

When we conducted the initial study in thirty-six schools we were impressed with the very great consistency of these 'academic' and 'expressive' profiles in the pupils' evaluations of their lessons. With a range of schools that took in the London docks as well as rural Devon, not to mention Bristol, Cambridge, and the Channel Islands, it was indeed surprising that the pupils should show such a remarkably consistent response to these evaluative statements. In point of fact when this larger and more representative sample of schools was used the profile for English was much more distinctly an 'academic' one. Figure 7 below gives the profiles for the endorsement of the six positive statements from that earlier study with fourth-year pupils in thirty-six schools. The schools comprised three direct-grant schools, one private school, six grammar schools, eighteen secondary modern schools, and eight comprehensive schools. There were 3,400 pupils in all. They were chosen to include single-sex and co-educational, urban and rural, large and small schools.

Naturally a comparison was made between the profiles of each

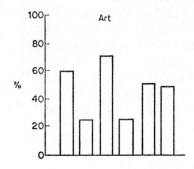
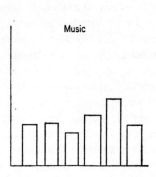

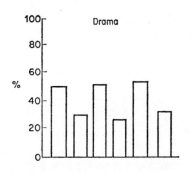

Six positive evaluative statements:
1. In my —— lessons there are lots of new and interesting things to do.
2. In my —— lessons I feel I have learned something important to me.
3. In my —— lessons, I am allowed to develop my own ideas and do things in my own way.
4. In my —— lessons I am told clearly what to do and how to do it.
5. My —— lessons are fun and I really enjoy myself.
6. In my —— lessons the teacher gives me all the help I need to improve my work.

FIG. 7 PUPIL EVALUATION OF 4 SUBJECTS—Pattern of responses in thirty-six schools, 4th year only

of the schools taken separately but although the amount of evaluation varied considerably among different types of school the shape of the evaluative responses (the two profiles, academic and expressive) did not. The implications of this are rather important. It would appear that despite differences in styles, curriculum provision, and personalities of teachers there is a remarkable uniformity of response in the way that the pupils define the subjects and evaluate them. At first glance it appears that the teacher is unable to alter the subject image in the mind of the pupils even though he may attract a greater or lesser degree of positive endorsement for each evaluative statement. However, this would be a misleading conclusion. Although it is undoubtedly true that very few teachers do change the subject image it most certainly does happen and even in this study there were one or two notable exceptions which we went on to investigate further. One of these exceptions concerned the teaching of English. In one of the thirty-six schools the profile for English teaching contradicted the others. It was essentially an expressive profile instead of an academic one. Figure 8 below compares the shape of the English profile for this one school with the average shape for all the others.

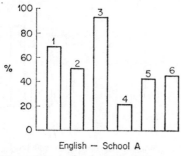 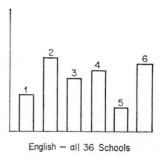

English — School A   English — all 36 Schools

Six positive evaluative statements:

1. In my ——— lessons there are lots of new and interesting things to do.
2. In my ——— lessons I feel I have learned something important to me.
3. In my ——— lessons, I am allowed to develop my own ideas and do things in my own way.
4. In my ——— lessons I am told clearly what to do and how to do it.
5. My ——— lessons are fun and I really enjoy myself.
6. In my ——— lessons the teacher gives me all the help I need to improve my work.

FIG. 8 PUPIL EVALUATION OF *ENGLISH* LESSON—Pattern of responses in thirty-six schools, 4th year only

The Pupils

Naturally we wanted to know something more about the reasons for this apparent contradiction. For this and other reasons this school was selected to be included among the six that we explored intensively in the second phase of the research. One of the advantages of this second phase was that the age range of the pupils was extended to include all of the school years. In this particular school the first three years are organised in integrated studies programmes (I.D.E.). In the fourth and fifth (and sixth) years subject teaching takes over. In these latter years English is taught by one teacher who is also the head of the department. There is a strongly expressive ambience throughout the school. The following comparison between the pupil's endorsements of the evaluative statements in the first three years as compared with the fourth and fifth years is very revealing.

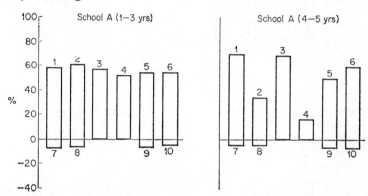

Ten evaluative statements:

1. In my —— lessons there are lots of new and interesting things to do
2. In my —— lessons I feel I have learned something important to me.
3. In my —— lessons, I am allowed to develop my own ideas and do things in my own way.
4. In my —— lessons I am told clearly what to do and how to do it.
5. My —— lessons are fun and I really enjoy myself.
6. In my —— lessons the teacher gives me all the help I need to improve my work.
7. In my —— lessons there are no new and interesting things to do.
8. In my —— lessons I feel I haven't learned anything important to me.
9. My —— lessons are boring and I don't enjoy myself.
10. In my —— lessons the teacher does not give me enough help to improve my work.

FIG. 9 PUPIL EVALUATION OF *ENGLISH* LESSON—Pattern of responses in School A, years 1–3 and years 4–5

It is apparent that in the first three years there is a remarkable uniformity in the pupils' responses to each evaluative statement. The expressive and academic attributes appear to be balanced in the pupils' responses. In the fourth and fifth year however when the head of the department takes over, the teaching of English reveals a strongly expressive profile with the notable exception that the pupils do feel that they are given a great deal of teacher

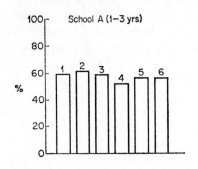

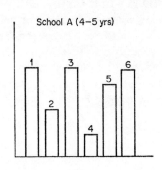

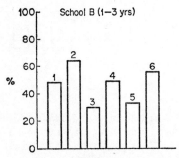

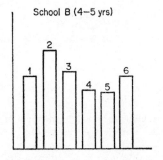

Six positive evaluative statements:

1. In my —— lessons there are lots of new and interesting things to do.
2. In my —— lessons I feel I have learned something important to me.
3. In my —— lessons, I am allowed to develop my own ideas and do things in my own way.
4. In my —— lessons I am told clearly what to do and how to do it.
5. My —— lessons are fun and I really enjoy myself.
6. In my —— lessons the teacher gives me all the help I need to improve my work.

FIG. 10 PUPIL EVALUATION OF *ENGLISH* LESSON—Pattern of responses in School A and School B, years 1–3 and years 4–5

support, more in fact than the first three years register. Nevertheless they no longer experience the subject as being anything like so
important and there is a very low endorsement of the statement on
being 'told clearly what to do and taught how to do it'. Before we
go on to suggest reasons for this expressive profile of English it
will be helpful to compare the responses of pupils in this school
for English with those of a matched school. We will refer to the
former as school A and the latter as school B.

In school A there was no definite profile for English in the
responses of the first three years whereas in school B, as can be seen,
there is a distinctly academic profile. In the fourth and fifth years
the academic profile is maintained in school B with one reversal,
namely that the pupils feel they are allowed to develop their own
ideas and they are not told as much as formerly what to do. In both
schools there is an increase in the amount of provision for English
that the pupils want as between the first three years and the last two.
In their building of a curriculum for 'the next ten school periods'
the pupils in school A allotted an average of 10% of their curriculum
to English in the first three years and 17% in the fourth and fifth
years. In school B the respective figures were 7% and 12½%. The
fact is, however, that the fourth and fifth years in school A endorse
the statements for English in a rather similar way to their endorsement of art and drama.

Although responses are high for such things as novelty and interest and self-expression they are low for importance and clear
direction. The fact that this teacher should produce a profile similar
in certain respects to an art profile is not so surprising perhaps when
one learns, as we did, that she was trained as an art teacher and did
in fact teach art before switching to English teaching. Her English
lessons were in any case conducted in an atmosphere strongly
reminiscent of the art room. Gone were the even rows of desks.
Instead there were lots of old armchairs and other pieces of furni-
ture littered untidily around the room. The atmosphere was pleasant, relaxed and decidedly non-academic. The expressive aspect
of English teaching was completely to the fore in the work of this
teacher. The pupils were involved in exercises that were virtually
invitations to 'paint' feeling with words. There was a tremendous
emphasis on the subjective power of words. Realised form was
introduced to the pupils in connection with creative writing exercises and there was no evidence whatever, in the lessons that we

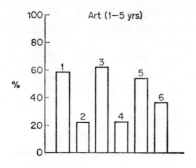

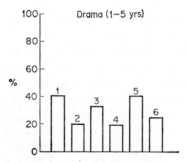 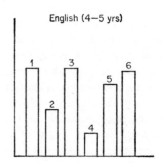

Six positive evaluative statements:

1. In my —— lessons there are lots of new and interesting things to do.
2. In my —— lessons I feel I have learned something important to me.
3. In my —— lessons, I am allowed to develop my own ideas and do things in my own way.
4. In my —— lessons I am told clearly what to do and how to do it.
5. My —— lessons are fun and I really enjoy myself.
6. In my —— lessons the teacher gives me all the help I need to improve my work.

FIG. 11 PUPIL EVALUATION OF 3 SUBJECTS—Pattern of responses in School A

observed, of the ubiquitous 'critic talk' of which so many English departments are proud.

Furthermore there is a very interesting and unusual aspect of the pupils' response to the statements on being 'told clearly what to do and taught how to do it' and on 'the teacher giving me all the help I need to improve my work'. Whereas these statements usually produce reasonably similar levels of response from the pupils they are clearly much more separated from one another in the responses of this teacher's pupils. In the first three years for example the endorsements for these statements were 55% and 51% respectively. In the fourth and fifth years however the corresponding figures are 62% and 17%. In the matched school, (school B) the endorsement of these two statements reveals only a very moderate divergence by comparison. In the first three years the figures are 56% and 50% and in the fourth and fifth years they are 53% and 43½% respectively. The divergence in school A between the pupils' endorsements for each of these statements (62% and 17%) is all the more remarkable when one realises that nothing like it occurred in any of our other schools *in respect of any subject*. In the great majority of cases the levels were very similar indeed (29 out of 36 comparisons revealed differences of 10% and under) and in many they were identical. In one or two cases there were divergences as high as 15% between the levels of endorsement for the two statements and in one instance only in the case of art lessons, the divergence reached 22% which is still less than half the 45% recorded in school A.

In the light of the argument developed throughout the book so far this divergence is of some interest. Being told clearly what to do and taught how to do it implies a considerable measure of rule-direction. In many cases pupils associate this with the teacher giving them enough help to improve their work, hence the close association in the levels of endorsement for these statements whether they are high, low, or average. The teacher of the fourth and fifth years in school A had most certainly relinquished rule-directed control of the medium in her teaching of the pupils. On the other hand she worked very strongly and intensively with what I have called reflexive control of the medium. She provided carefully selected material to stimulate feeling-impulse in the pupils and guided their exploration of the expressive possibilities of the medium to release it. Exercises in which the pupils engaged were carefully phased so that the teacher might enter the process and join the pupil in the expressive act at any of several natural stages of the exercise if that was needed to keep the pupil in control of the medium. Because of this phasing of the exercise and the creative partnership with the teacher, the pupils felt that they were actually going somewhere and that the work had point to it. Furthermore they were able to obtain a great deal of direct feedback in the very process of building an idea. The phasing was not determined by rules about using

language but by the teacher's intuitive grasp of the natural stages in the transformation of a feeling-impulse to a feeling-idea. It is this natural phasing that enabled the teacher to develop reflexive control of the medium in the pupil, thereby keeping feeling-impulse and medium closely identified.

It is therefore perfectly natural that these pupils should endorse the teacher as providing a great deal of help to improve their work while not agreeing that they are told clearly what to do and taught how to do it. What they might be said to be endorsing is a lack of rule-direction and a sufficiency of reflexive control. Certainly I believe this to be the case, although there is as yet insufficient evidence to be sure of it.

When we interviewed these pupils some very interesting responses came to light. It was apparent that the pupils not only enjoyed their English lessons but they felt that the lessons really did something for them personally. Nevertheless there was widespread anxiety that these were not 'proper English lessons' in the respectable academic sense. The pupils were concerned about acquiring socially acceptable educational credentials, and one or two confessed to going down to the technical college in the evening for tuition in 'proper English lessons'. The irony of the situation was that this teacher was able to put into practice many of the ideals which her colleagues in other English departments approve in theory. In so doing however she violated the academic image of English. The girls registered this in the evaluative statements by producing only a 35% endorsement for the statement 'I feel I have learned something important to me' as compared with a 72% endorsement by the fourth and fifth years in the matched school (school B).

No more than a glimpse has been provided in the above discussion of the data that we collected in respect of pupil response. At the present time a fairly thoroughgoing statistical analysis of the data is under way and this should throw some light on at least the 'crude' factors at work in determining pupil response. The few aggregate comparisons based upon two sections of a questionnaire, that I have presented here, comprise only some of the comparisons that might have been made. My purpose has been to develop an argument using the data for illustrative purposes. The roots of the argument are very complex indeed and are much more broadly based in my own consciousness than in the research programme. Nevertheless the data has undoubtedly transformed the argument as it has unfolded in a way that is analogous at least to the transformation brought about by the oscillation in consciousness between feeling-impulse and medium which I have held to characterise the art process. I have used the data from our interviews, questionnaires and observations very much as a medium in which to build an idea.

From the various types of contact established with the conscious-ness of pupils and teachers alike a picture has been built up of some of the cumulative pressures of the academic system. The pupil is increasingly caught in a number of contradictory tendencies which, if they are not soon resolved, will in all probability build up into a reservoir of impotence and resentment in the face of a society that is making increasing demands on his ingenuity and motivation without preparing him adequately to meet them. Teachers every-where are seeing signs of this already. In order to respond with sufficient motivation and sufficient flexibility to meet the demands of the modern world the pupil needs to participate actively in his own development in a way that is denied by the traditional approaches to teaching academic subjects which are still the funda-mental basis of our entire educational system despite advances in curriculum thinking.

Learning is a process of discovery. When a man is taken by the arm here and there at the behest of an insistent guide, and is told what to look at and what its bearings are in relation to other things he has been shown, he does not feel very much like an explorer making a discovery. He probably feels safe but bored. If he should then meet another man who says, 'Make discoveries, explore the possibilities, find your own way,' he will in all probability feel excited but too scared to embark, precisely because he has had little experience of thinking for himself. One solution that might imme-diately commend itself is to become a sly man, one of life's own tourists. Then he will move where he wants to move but only if the guide book says it is in order to do so. A tourist is sly because he cheats. He pretends to make discoveries while he is busy copying the answers out of the guide book. He is stupid, too. Who can be more stupid than a man who cheats by robbing himself of his own possibilities for experience?

This is the dilemma of so many of our adolescents. They run from the irrelevance of the academic dogmas which deny them the fruits of participation and discovery and yet they are forced by their very training to cling tenaciously to the rule book even when expressing themselves, otherwise they feel no respect for the validity of their own actions. The objective, the logical, the rational, all are experienced as ominously threatening to the adolescent, the more so because of his great dependence upon them. He knows if he leans hard enough they will break, and he lacks the intelligence of feeling which alone can guarantee his survival when they do.

8 From Within The Expressive Act

In this final part, I will attempt to formulate, from the general framework of Part One, and from our experience in schools as interpreted in Part Two, an approach to the resolving of the fundamental contradictions of arts teaching. These arise from the fact that arts curricula and arts teaching frequently remain external to the pupil's expressive acts. To the extent that the creative process itself is not comprehended in the praxis of teachers, their praxis cannot become involved in the pupil's expressive act, and that is where it needs to be if it is to play any kind of effective rôle in developing and realising the pupil's potential to use form to organise sensate experience. The arts teacher all too frequently finds himself vacillating between the extremes of facilitating and inhibiting self-expression, caught up in irrelevant criteria for differentiating between the 'legitimate' and the 'non-legitimate', and rationalising his practice in ways that often lead to the opposite of what he intends with respect to self-expression.

The quality of the child's sensate experience is the most fundamental aspect of subject-reflexive action (this is the term that I will now substitute for 'self-expression'). It is the child's direct sensing that both guides and controls the expressive act until it is recalled in an expressive form, a feeling-form. The teacher needs to enter the creative process from the outset, from its very inception. He needs to initiate the sensate experience in the child that is to be the motive power of the expression that follows. Of course it might be objected at once that because the child's sensate experience is unique to him, for the teacher to enter the creative process from the outset is something of a contradiction in terms. This is not so, however, for such an objection fails to comprehend the nature of the sensate problem. The sensate problem that arises in the evocation of direct sensate experience is really compounded of two aspects. In the first place, sensate experience makes demands upon the individual to structure it. This structuring can be described in terms of the relationships between sensory elements that are an invariant aspect of the functioning of all human beings. In other words, sensory elements are organised in terms of contrasts, semblances, harmonies, discords, etc., regardless of their content, the 'stuff' of which they are made. I shall have more to say about these invariant aspects of sensate ordering shortly. For the moment, we need only observe that this part of the sensate problem can be conceived of as *generality*. It concerns the structuring or ordering of sensate experience, and this makes use of the same basic relationships from one individual to another. The second aspect, however, concerns the stuff or content of the sensate experience in which these relationships occur. While the principles of ordering sensate experience are the same from one individual to another, the content of the sensate experience is not. Each individual's experience is unique to him, it is his *particularity*.

We are now in a position to state what is meant by a sensate problem. Quite simply all sensate disturbance whether great or small, pleasant or unpleasant, is a problem in so far as it makes demands upon us to structure our particularity. If the teacher wishes to set a sensate problem, therefore, he must evoke sensate experience that makes demands upon the pupil to structure his particularity. Since the teacher does not have access to the particularity of the pupil he can only enter the expressive act of the pupil through the demands that he makes in respect of structuring. In other words, he can enter the pupil's expressive act through its generality by controlling and developing the structural demands made in respect of the pupil's unique experience.

In order to pursue the matter on a more practical level I will discuss the teaching of the creative arts in terms of three phases of the creative process that I hold to be invariant. They are the 'setting of the sensate problem', the 'making of a holding form', and the 'movement through successive approximations to a resolution'. A word of caution is necessary, however. In none of the illustrations or examples that are used to describe these phases of the creative process in the teaching context, is there any attempt to provide possible material for curricula. The examples are for the most part quite inappropriate from that point of view. They have been constructed to illustrate what I mean by the phases of the creative process when used within a teaching context, but they have no other value.

1 The setting of the sensate problem

As I have stated, all sensate experience is a sensate problem in so far as it makes demands upon the individual to structure his particularity. If the teacher simply evokes sensate experience in the pupil of any kind, the pupil has a sensate problem. He needs to structure his unique experience and that requires the use of an expressive medium in which subject-reflexive action can take place. However, just to evoke sensate experience is not enough if the teacher is to have any part in the development of the pupil's expressive act. He needs to know from a structural point of view just what kind of problem he is setting. In other words he needs to have conceptualised the structural characteristics, the generality of the problem, before he sets it (by evoking it) within the particularity of the pupil's experience.

The stimulus forms that the teacher uses to set the sensate problem—i.e. the forms that he uses to evoke a 'contrast' such as that between the warm and the cool or a 'dialectic' such as that between love and hate—have the status of 'realised form' even though they may not be works of art. Whenever realised form is used, the teacher needs to ensure that it does not inhibit or dominate the pupil's creative expression. When using realised form to set the sensate problem, therefore, the teacher may find it helpful to incorporate certain safeguards. The object of the exercise is to set the problem in the particularity of the pupil's own experience, and it is this particularity which should be the 'stuff' of his expressive form. To assist the pupil to transcend the particular forms that the teacher uses to evoke the sensate problem, there are three courses of action that appear to be appropriate.

In the first place it will help if the teacher makes use of different iconic media from that in which the pupil's expressive act is taking place. In other words if the pupil is going to work in a verbal medium then the teacher might find it helpful to set the sensate problem using visual and/or auditory icons. This use of a different sensate modality in the stimulus situation from the one in which the child is expressing himself not only serves to reduce the dominance of the stimulus form, it encourages a greater awareness of the range and possibilities of iconic languages. The pupil comes more easily to comprehend the relationship between feeling and form and to assimilate the iconic as a distinct mode of knowing.

In addition to varying the sensate modality of the stimulus forms to distance it from the expressive forms of the pupil, the teacher might find it helpful to use a number of quite different stimulus forms to evoke the same sensate problem. In this way the pupil is able to transcend the particular forms used to set the problem by grasping the resemblance between the different forms, the 'gestalt' they have in common. The 'warm-cool' contrast can be presented in a variety of different forms. Different though the forms would be, they would each possess the same central principle of sensate ordering; the same 'gestalt' (i.e. the warm-cool contrast) and it would be this gestalt that would become embedded in the particularity of the pupil's experience. The setting of the sensate problem is the evoking of a specific gestalt, a sensate ordering in the context of the pupil's experience. The range and variety of different stimulus forms both release the pupil from too great a dependence on any single form, and at the same time encourage him to deepen and widen his exploration of his own experience. 'Sweet-sorrowing' is a sensate experience at quite a high level of complexity. It can be evoked by any number of different stimulus situations apart from the most obvious. Once it has been evoked directly, the elements of sweet-sorrowing are sensate experience. They constitute a sensate problem, transcending the particular forms through which it was evoked.

It must not be forgotten, however, that the abstraction of the gestalt in the particularity of the pupil's experience is achieved through the pupil's own expressive act. If this is not to become focused upon the form that evoked the sensate problem (as it is in art appreciation) then the teacher must make use of stimulus forms, the particularities of which are relevant to areas of the pupil's particularity that are *not* engaged in his subsequent expressive act. In order to be evoked at all the sensate problem must be presented in stimulus forms that are relevant to the pupil's experience. It is here that the teacher's own sensitivity to the sensate experience of the children he teaches will be his best guide. Dirt and sudden surprise evoke quite different sensate experiences in a child who lives in a slum from those which they evoke in a child who lives in a neat suburban street. The teacher must be sensitive to these differences if he is to have any hope of planting the seeds of the same gestalt in contrasting soils. Nevertheless, although the particularity of the stimulus form must be relevant to the same part of the child's particularity in order that he can respond to it, the teacher needs to engage a different part of the child's particularity in the expressive act that follows. Only in this way can the pupil free himself entirely from the particularity of the stimulus forms and go on to create an expressive form of his own as an original expressive act. Thus the sensate experience of desolation evoked through the particularity of natural scenery can be expressed through the particularity of human relationships, or urban streets. The more the teacher is able to distance the evoking stimulus form from the pupil's expressive form, while at the same time ensuring that both are within the compass of the pupil's particularity, the more deeply will the pupil be able to realise the creative possibilities of the sensate problem as set by the teacher. At the same time the teacher's praxis will be maintained within the pupil's expressive act for he will have a hold on its generality.

Even where realised form is not used as the original stimulus form but is presented for appreciation, it should always be integrated into the creative activity of the pupils. It should form part of a cycle of creative expression which begins with the setting of the sensate problem followed by the child's expressive form. Realised form for appreciation can then be presented as a 'centrepiece' which the pupil will be motivated to explore because of its relationship to his own creative act. Finally, the exploration of these possibilities can be used to give rise to new creative expression on the part of the pupil. In what follows, however, we will be concerned with the use of realised form as the original stimulus form for the setting of the sensate problem and not with the use of realised form for appreciation.

We can pursue the matter more concretely. Supposing that a group of pupils are expressing themselves in verbal form, the teacher might well use visual and auditory stimulus materials in which to set his problem. He will find it helpful if he can involve the pupils in collecting and selecting these once they have begun to grasp the nature of his problem. In the case of the warm-cool contrast there are many possibilities that suggest themselves in the juxtaposition of warm and cool light, of textures and colours, of natural scenes and the shapes of objects, of the eyes of people and the surfaces of buildings and roads, of warm and cool tones in jazz, of footsteps in a city, and of natural sounds. In each case the warm-cool contrast must be central and it must be evoked directly with the minimum of discursive explanation or analysis from the teacher.

In the case of the love-hate dialectic the teacher might again make use of dramatic visual and auditory stimulus material (N.B. actual visual and auditory material is implied here and not simply verbal reference to such material). The Romeo and Juliet theme of *West Side Story* and Tchaikovsky's *Fantasia* suggest themselves; any visual or auditory images that convey the emergence of love within a context of hate and the emergence of hate within a context of love. Religious images and myth provide a rich source of material. Pictures of mothers and babies in the holocaust of war, a lovers' quarrel, etc. There is probably no dialectic more intensely explored in human culture. Nevertheless, the teacher should be careful to select stimulus forms that have the dialectic or contrast or whatever as their gestalt rather than those in which these structures appear as non-essential features.

A drama teacher, on the other hand, might work somewhat differently getting the pupils to work up a flow of expressive images in words. He might make them establish the warm-cool contrast in sound and stimulate their imaginations to encompass texture, colour, the lines of faces and gestures, etc. The problem cannot be regarded as having been set until the contrast or dialectic or harmony or whatever, is a felt experience of some intensity. The same applies of course to the music teacher or the art teacher.

The sensate problem is a sensate disturbance with certain 'structural' characteristics. It is the structural characteristics of the disturbance that constitute the generality of the sensate problem. If the teacher is to enter the creative process at the outset and to devise curricula in a meaningful way then his conception of these structural characteristics becomes of central importance. He needs (ultimately) to formulate curriculum objectives in terms of them in order to enhance the pupil's progressive mastery of new and more complex levels of sensate experience. The teacher, therefore, needs a scheme for conceptualising the structuring of sensate disturbance and its development.

As was stated in Chapter 2, adequate feeling response in this sense refers solely to the universalistic and invariant modes of functioning of the individual in respect of sensate experience. His particularity is something that he creates in self-expression but not solely in self-expression. He creates it in every choice that he makes, in every action that follows impulse. The curriculum therefore does not determine the child's Being, his particularity, but it plays a very large part in the development of the child's *mode* of functioning in respect of the world.

How then shall we conceive of the development of this invariant mode of functioning with regard to sensate experience? In the absence of specific explanatory research in this area we can at least steer a tentative course by staying close to the basic epistemological framework developed by Jean Piaget. We can do this by proposing a parallel development of sensate experience to the one that he proposes with regard to the development of logical thought. The earliest phase of this development would correspond to Piaget's stage of 'sensory motor' behaviour. The infant's sensing is directly in relation to objects that he encounters. It is non-representational, and sensate experience lacks the locus of organisation independent of the object itself to be truly 'operational'.

Later on we can identify a second stage corresponding to Piaget's 'concrete operations'. Here the individual's sensing is in relation to his sensing of objects and is therefore one stage removed from the objects themselves. This corresponds to the 'operations upon operations' that characterised the behaviour of the young mathematician acquiring the concept of conservation of number in the illustration given in Chapter 1. At this level the child is not simply sensing objects but is actively sensing his sensing of objects. He is using iconic symbols in order to do this. Sensate experience of objects gives rise eventually to iconic representation. Through the use of iconoc symbols sensing can be made to operate upon sensing.

The use of symbol is very important here. At the outset of this developmental stage the symbols are closely identified with the objects themselves. Because the child finds it impossible to distinguish them clearly from one another, his use of iconic symbols bears the imprint of the free play of sensation. He has not yet built up stable and independent organisations of iconic symbols that will control his sensing. As time goes by, however, such stable symbol organisations do emerge until at about the age of eight he is beginning to use very consistent and stable iconic themas to order and control his sensate experience. While these are clearly distinguishable from the object world that they represent, they are still very much tied to it in the eight-year-old's experience. He is still not operating at more than one level removed from the world of objects. In other words he is not yet operating upon a level which is purely symbolic and in which he is not directly in contact with objects at all. When this occurs at around the age of eleven he enters into the stage of 'symbolic operations' characteristic of adolescent and post-adolescent abstractions. Now for the first time he recognises the universes of symbol and object as truly separate from one another. This complete separation of symbol and object gives rise to two consequences. At first there is something of a *representational crisis*. As the child comes to know the worlds of symbol and object as two different universes the relationship between them becomes a focus of special concern. He becomes increasingly self-conscious about his use of all expressive forms. All of those stable themas of late childhood now seem hideously inappropriate to represent reality. He discovers that they do not picture reality at all well. He is painfully aware that he is loaded up with expressive forms that will not do what he now sees as the function of expressive forms, namely to be 'realistic'. He has the photographic image on the brain. He no longer 'draws', he 'scribbles'; he no longer sings, he 'croaks'; he cannot make himself understood nor can he convey what he knows of the world. When the 'umbilical' cord between symbol and reality is finally cut he is no longer innocent, but responsible for the relationship between them. At first he tries desperately to identify them, to see in the symbol world a mirror for reality. As he gains in confidence, however, the true power of symbolic representation begins to dawn upon his actions. His symbolic operations reveal to him that he can not only represent all of the possibilities of objects in the world of symbols but he can reorganise them on a symbolic level thereby giving rise to new 'realities'. He ceases to concern himself so slavishly with objects and himself as object and looks increasingly to the possibilities for symbolic reorganisations and transformations of the 'real'. Symbolic abstraction begins in earnest. The process of symbolic abstraction which finally removed the symbol from reality and gave rise to the representational crisis, actually overcomes that crisis as it becomes increasingly stabilised.

It is important to bear in mind, however, that in the development I have sketched for sensate experience, I am referring to a parallel order to Piaget's genetic sequence and not to the same order. The two are as distinct from one another as subject-knowing is from object-knowing. In the case of symbolic operations, for example, Piaget's use of the term abstraction refers to the 'generalising' abstraction, the abstraction that subsumes reality. Symbolic abstraction in sensate experience is the exact opposite of this. It is an 'individualising' abstraction. It does not subsume anything at all. It 'crystallises' sensate experience in a unitary individualisation. I will make no attempt here to present my views on the nature of sensate abstraction but the following illustration might serve to point up the essential difference. When we speak of 'mother-hood' as a generalising abstraction, the category of 'motherhood' subsumes each and every instance of what we might term mothering behaviour, etc. When the artist succeeds in depicting 'motherhood' in a painting, however, he does not subsume anything at all. He crystallises a unitary sensate form through which 'motherhood' in all its *particularity* can be known. The generalising abstraction is a 'container' for reality (Rudolph Arnheim, *Visual Thinking*) whereas the individualising abstraction represents the very 'essence' of the individual's sensate experience.

Both types of symbolic abstraction, individualising and generalising, are 'holistic'. The generalising abstraction subsumes the totality of instances of reality in its domain. The individualising abstraction is an absorption, a crystallisation, of the totality of the individual's sensate experiences in its domain. The higher the level of generality in abstraction the wider the area subsumed. Similarly the higher the level of individualisation in abstraction, the greater is the range of sensate experiences absorbed in it. In their highest forms they give rise to the universal applicability of science and the universal appeal of art.

The organisation of symbols in terms of 'wholes' is what charac-terises symbolic abstraction of both types. These 'wholes' either subsume the totality of subjects in their domain or they 'absorb' the totality of sensate experiences in their domain. It is the latter type of whole with which we shall be concerned here. As a first crude approximation to a scheme for analysing sensate development, I will distinguish between the pre-adolescent phase in which symbol and object world are still tied to one another and in which symbolic organisation does not therefore assume a holistic form, and the adolescent (and post-adolescent) phase in which symbol is progressively freed from object and becomes independently organised to 'absorb' the totality of sensate experience in its domain.

In the pre-adolescent phase I will distinguish four operations in terms of which the ordering of sensate experience can be described.

1. *Contrasts*—the interplay of sensations one upon another can often be ordered by 'contrast'. Sensations in relation to the same sensate dimension contrast with one another as do black and white. They set each other off, and their very relativity highlights the distinctive features of each. Contrasts range from the simple ones arising out of direct encounters with objects, to very complex ones established at quite high levels of iconic organisation. Contrasts are really the counterpart of the operation of subtraction in mathematics. They capture the subtractive tension between sensate elements, the movement, the process, as it were, whereas the operation of subtraction conveys only structural transformations. The rough and the smooth, the hard and the gentle, the subtle contrasts between shapes and colour, all are the experiencing of individualising sensate differences. The elements in a subtraction, on the other hand, are generalising abstractions that subsume reality.

2. *Semblances*—the interplay of sensations on a sensate dimension can also be ordered in respect of their 'semblance' to one another instead of their contrasting with one another. Bright red can recall bright yellow. Thunder can recall the loud voice as can the pale shadow its darker form. The ordering of sensate elements by semblance is the counterpart of the operation of addition. Again it is the tension, the build-up between sensate elements that is crystallised in the semblance and not a structural transformation. It is the living additive quality in the interplay of sensations that we experience as semblance. As with contrasts, semblances can be simple or complex depending upon our level of symbolic operation.

3. *Harmonies*—sometimes sensate events blend together, like a rhyme in poetry, and emerge as a unitary sensate experience. The separate notes of a musical chord or the blends between shapes and colours fall into this category. When sensations are 'harmonised' in this way the operation is the counterpart of the mathematical operation of multiplication, and just as multiplication is really allied to addition so harmony is allied to semblance.

4. *Discords*—sensate events may be ordered in terms of their conflict with one another. Colours that clash, sounds that grate together, all sensate events that push each other apart, that fight each other, come into this category. 'Discord' is the counterpart of the operation of division in mathematics and just as division is closely allied to subtraction so discords are closely allied to contrasts. Discords, too, can range from the simple to the iconically complex.

When we come to consider adolescent development it is possible to distinguish four sensate operations that are higher-level counterparts of the four we have described already. These four all have one thing in common, namely that they all describe ordering in sensate experience at the level of the sensate totality. It is ordering in respect of 'wholes' rather than ordering between individual sensate events.

5. *Polarities*—when sensate events emerge from *a continuum of contrasts* then we can order them in terms of a 'polarity'. Clearly polarities are related to contrasts but whereas the latter consist of an ordering between elements, the polarity is the ordering of contrasts in relation to a sensate continuum, or sensate whole. To use a polarity to order sensate events implies that the individual has a grasp of the sensate continuum of contrasts that constitutes it.

6. *Identities*—when sensate events emerge from a continuum of semblances then we can order them in terms of an 'identity'. An identity is thus related to a semblance, but at the higher level of organisation of wholes. Sensate events cannot be ordered as identities unless the individual is able to use the sensate continuum of semblance in relation to which they emerge as identities.

7. *Syntheses*—when a totality of individual sensate events can be absorbed into a sensate whole we have a 'synthesis' in respect of which we can bind particular sensate events. Syntheses are the higher-level equivalent of harmonies.

8. *Dialectics*—when sensate contradictions and sensate divisions emerge within wholes we have a 'dialectic'. This is the higher-level equivalent of the discord. The individual is able to use a dialectic to order sensate events only if he can grasp the sensate whole in relation to which they contradict one another.

The scheme outlined above is really a very tentative outline of a system for classifying sensate experience. It is not a proper developmental sequence in that there is no attempt to define stages or levels or types of sensate themas beyond the crude distinction between the holistic requirements of purely symbolic functioning and the non-holistic requirements of pre-adolescent sensate experience. I have said nothing of the way in which we might combine our categories to produce the sensate equivalents of the logical systems that Piaget describes. I have concentrated instead on identifying what appear to me to be fundamental bases of order in sensate experience. Further exploration of these is beyond the scope of the present work. They are presented in their present form in the hope that they may spark off ideas in the minds of teachers for ordering curriculum objectives in the creative arts in relation to personal development. They have the advantage of being of general applicability to all of the creative arts and they provide a conception of the different levels of complexity of sensate problems and of the equivalence between sensate problems of the same level of complexity.

Once the teacher is able to formulate his curriculum objectives in the creative arts by making use of the structural properties of sensate experience he can bring to his work a coherence and relevance to the personal development of the pupil that will realise the most ambitious hopes of those who have pleaded for generations the case for the arts in education. To succeed in entering the creative process from the outset and involving his praxis within the pupil's self-expression, the teacher must be able to formulate the structural characteristics, the generality, of the sensate problem and he must embody these in forms that he can use to set the problem in the particularity of the pupil's sensate experience. When the problem is grasped as a felt reality by the pupil then the motive power of the creative act is there and the next stage begins at once.

2 The making of a holding form

Once the sensate problem has been set in the consciousness of the pupil as felt disturbance the expressive act that is to realise that disturbance can begin. An expressive act, however, takes place in time, and sensate experience does not stand still for its duration. If the individual does not encapsulate the sensate impulse then it will quickly dissolve in other sensate disturbances. For a problem to be resolved it needs to be held for the duration of the process of resolving it. As soon as the sensate problem is set the individual must establish a 'holding form' for it. In reality this often follows so closely upon the evocation of the sensate problem that it is usually indistinguishable from its consciousness. Nevertheless, it is a vital part of the creative process and without it the sensate problem itself would change out of all recognition and defy resolution. One cannot resolve so volatile and protean an event as a sensate disturbance unless one encapsulates it in a holding form.

The holding form is merely the seed of which the full expressive form is the flower. A writer may encapsulate the essential sensate impulse of a whole book in a title. If the title preceded the writing of the book then it may well have been used as a holding form. Consider the titles *Great Expectations* or *Dead Souls*. One can well imagine that such titles might have served as holding forms for their authors to capture the essential idea, the kernel of inspiration, which receives its full expression in the books that follow. I cannot say, of course, whether these titles were used in that way but something like them, whether in words or visual form or musical motif, must have preceded the books themselves in the consciousness of the authors.

The effectiveness of a holding form depends upon its complete simplicity, its 'minimal' character. *Its purpose is to encapsulate only the essential movement of the sensate impulse and to hold that movement in consciousness for the duration of the expressive act.* As I have already argued, the sensate problem itself consists of the structure of sensate disturbance which I have described in terms of 'contrasts', 'discords', 'identities', etc. When it has been set in the particularity of the individual's experience the individual produces a form that captures these structural characteristics in their barest essentials. It is the essential gestalt of the disturbance that is held in the holding form. If the latter is 'fussy' or imposes non-essential features then it will only serve to confuse the act of expression that follows. Because the holding form is often instantaneously produced and contains the vitality, the inspiration of the full expression, the latter being as the oak in the acorn, so creativity itself is often spoken of as instantaneous, a 'flash of inspiration'.

Naturally, any expressive medium can be used to make a holding form. A sequence of gestures, a certain rhythm or pitch sequence, etc. In one school that we researched I actually encountered a head of an art department who had intuitively arrived at the notion that the making of such an initial form was an invaluable aid to the creative process in the teaching situation. His was the only example that I myself came across of the explicit use of what I have termed the making of a holding form, in the teaching situation. All of the older pupils began their creative expression in this way.

'So what we tend to do is to get them to decide on some abstract theme, to choose a theme like growth or progress or destruction, something like that. *Then we get them to make a symbol for it and that seems somehow to switch them on to thinking in the right free sort of way* and from then on they can do anything which relates to the theme but we hope everything they do relates to the theme they have symbolised . . . so they all produce their symbols but from then they're on their own. And they can use anything they can find in the department . . . I am not quite sure how it happens but it does seem to work.'

If the teacher involves the pupils in making some sort of holding form then he can monitor his own success in setting the sensate problem. Differing children should produce different holding forms depending upon their particular sensate experience but all forms should embody the structural characteristics, the contrasts or semblances, etc., that constituted the sensate problem. Perhaps the teacher might find it helpful to get the pupil to produce two or more 'equivalent' holding forms. In any case, for the teacher to maintain his praxis within the pupil's self-expression, contact with the pupil's holding form prior to its elaboration in a full expression is a distinct advantage. It permits the teacher to exercise the teaching function at a very early stage in the time sequence of the expressive act.

Of course, the holding form does not prevent the sensate impulse from undergoing changes in the process of reverberation set up within the individual in the actual creative act, but the holding form preserves the integrity, the gestalt of the sensate impulse throughout these changes. If it fails to do so then the individual must either abandon the expressive act or break the seal of the holding form and create a new holding form with a new gestalt.

When the holding form is used as an explicit part of the educational encounter, the teacher can use it to help the pupil establish control over the idea. The next phase of the creative process

enables the teacher to help the pupil establish control over the
medium in which he is working.

3 The movement through successive approximations to a resolution

The pupil's respect for his expressive act vanishes when he loses
control of the medium. The greatest threat to his control of the
medium occurs when the oscillation in consciousness between
impulse and medium results in the two sensings (outgoing and
incoming) being too far apart to set up any kind of effective reverberation, and consequently there is no effective guidance for further
expressive behaviour. The pupil is then unable to create an expressive form that *recalls* his sensing. He is unable to guide his sensate
impulse effectively through the expressive medium. The problem
exists to the extent that the expressive task demands a finer degree
of control than the individual can manage. He needs to work up
to that refinement of control. The teacher can enable him to do this
by conceiving of the same task in terms of a series of successive
approximations to a resolution of the sensate problem. The approximations would be such that the earliest in the series would be
relatively crude and as the series progressed they would become
gradually more refined. The important point is that a resolution
of a sensate problem can be worked up in a number of different
approximations ranging at one extreme from a form that contains
the gestalt of the problem but which requires only relatively crude
management of the medium, to the other extreme where much finer
controls are required to produce a much more refined resolution
of the sensate problem. In other words the structural characteristics
of the problem remain throughout. Its gestalt does not alter from
one approximation to another. It is the same gestalt that is embodied
in the holding form, but in managing each approximation the
individual is engaged in working up a resolution of the problem into
a full expression. He is progressing from gross to refined control of
the medium in respect of the same problem. The task has not been
divided up like a cake into separate and distinct pieces. It is not a
case of saying, 'Now we have completed this part, we will begin
upon a different one.' Rather the integrity of the task has been
preserved in every version of it that the teacher has evolved in the
series. These versions all incorporate the structural characteristics

of the problem but they differ in the demands they make upon the individual in respect of control of the medium.

Let us imagine that a child is attempting to work with paints to convey an attitude of joy. Let us suppose further that he is using human figures to establish the joyous attitude. Without intending to presume how best to organise a series of successive approximations we can at least imagine the following possibilities to illustrate the process. The teacher might begin by requiring the pupils to produce the joyous attitude using only coloured 'stick men' forms until he is satisfied that the pupil has explored to the full the possibilities for conveying the joyous attitude in the angles and relationships of the sticks and their colours. He might then get them to experiment with expressing the joyous attitude not in stick men but in the rough basic outlines of human figures which they colour to enhance the joy expressed in the postural relationships. In the next approximation the pupils might build up a picture of human figures making use of crude textural gradients and contrasts. The series might progress in a number of different ways perhaps culminating in figures whose joyous attitude is conveyed not only in terms of the larger features of body posture and colour but also in terms of the finer features of facial expression, dress and textural gradient. The point is that each approximation is complete in itself. Each is a version of the same basic problem, that of using visual representations of human figures to express joy in all its contrasts, semblances, etc. The difference between them lies in the demands that each makes in respect of control of the medium. These demands are increased as the approximations approach a full expression. A quite different way of proceeding would have been to break the task up into a sequence of stages, each distinct from the next. For example the teacher might start with the face and then go on to deal with the body, etc. However this kind of differentiation in the task is precisely what is *not* meant by the method of 'successive approximations to a resolution'.

The art teacher would no doubt be able to find much better and more relevant instances to illustrate my point than I have provided in the example given above. It was necessary that I should give some concrete illustration to picture what I meant by successive approximations to a resolution but I have done this without intending to imply that the example constitutes a good or satisfactory solution to a problem in the art lesson. This was simply a possible organisation serving to illustrate the idea behind the method. When the pupil uses expressive action to realise his feeling-impulse he often needs to work up to the expression but it is vital that he does not lose the wholeness of his sensate problem, of his feeling-impulse while he is doing so. He must preserve this through each 'working' of the medium and the only way that he can do that is to ensure that each 'working' of the medium is an integral approximation of his task. By successive approximations in which finer and still finer medium control is instituted he proceeds towards further realisation of his feeling impulse. The oscillation between the impulse and its effect in the medium is rendered possible throughout the expressive behaviour and it is this oscillation, this reflexive control which is guarding the individual's response. The method of successive approximations simply ensures that the individual's impulse remains in contact with its effect in the medium and therefore that reverberation between them can take place.

This gradual working up of the expressive form through a series of approximations enables the pupil to remain reflexively in control of the medium; to maintain unbroken the contact between sensate impulse for release and the expressive medium in which it is to be released. Too often the two become separated, either because the pupil's task is quite beyond him, or because he is in the habit of planning, in some technical way, the construction of the form in isolation from the impulse that is guiding the expressive act. In either case there are only two possible results. The pupil must simply lose control of the medium or establish rule-directed control of the medium. To establish reflexive control the pupil requires to use his sensate impulse to initiate a movement of successive

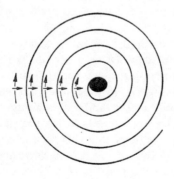

approximations to a resolution of that impulse. We might represent this process as one of circling inwards (or spiralling inwards) from the outer ranges of relatively crude approximation through progressively more refined approximations until the 'resolution form' is reached at the centre.

We start with a broad sweep at the form which moves into a more refined sweep, etc., until we hit the expressive form accurately in the highly controlled movement at the centre. Obviously, in practice, the range and speed of the accomplishment of successive approximations will vary from individual to individual and from situation to situation. It will vary too with the nature of the problem. A good marksman is one for whom the range of successive approximations is narrow and the speed of movement through approximations is like lightning. Ideally the teacher should develop in his pupils the method of working in successive approximations rather than imposing upon them particular sequences of approximations for a given piece of work. In other words the pupil should be able to work up his own successive approximations to a resolution in accordance with his specific needs provided he has learned the method properly and preserves the essential gestalt through each approximation in the series. If he loses that then he breaks the contact between impulse and medium which is the whole point of the exercise. The teacher might find it helpful to impose successive approximations in the phasing of the creative task when the pupil is exploring a new or unfamiliar technique or medium in relation to his sensate impulse. In this case the teacher would simply be phasing the task in ways that ensured that the pupil's successive approximations explored the full range of possibilities in the medium. Once the principle has been grasped it can be applied in specific situations in whatever ways are necessary for maximum effectiveness.

Let us imagine an English lesson in which pupils are working with the warm-cool contrast as a sensate problem. The pupils might first of all work up an organisation of warm-cool word sounds that they can juxtapose to produce the contrast without paying any attention to syntax or meaning. They might then work with the same contrast in word sounds plus rhythms again without paying attention to syntax or meaning. The pupils might then phase in syntax and meaning by making use of warm and cool verbs and then by working up the form to a fully meaningful statement.

Again I must stress that the use of the principle depends upon the specific encounter and the parties to that encounter. Children with a great facility for the expressive use of language may not require to use such overt and wide-ranging approximations. If they have a true 'feel' for words they will move swiftly through a range of covert and finely shaded approximations. Many—if not most—pupils, do not have such a feel for words, and their inhibitions in the construction of meaningful speech units lead to an undue obsession with the formal structure of speech, its syntax. This denies them the very control that they seek. It is rather like trying to paint pictures by rules or compose music by formulae. In the truly expressive act the movement is always from sensate impulse to form. Successive approximations must always remain closely bound to the sensate impulse. When words are used expressively their referential meanings should grow out of their expressive function. The 'feel' for words as sound and rhythm meanings should appear earlier in the sequence of successive approximations than the feel for words as referential meanings (i.e. in the sense of dictionary meanings). This is not to underestimate the importance of referential meaning in expression. On the contrary the organisation of word meanings involves the very finest level of medium control and it is for this reason that the pupil who has little 'feel' for words might well benefit from working inwards, releasing his sensate impulse first in word sounds, then perhaps sound plus rhythm, etc., until word meanings are introduced and he is able to construct a much more refined and elaborate verbal form for his gestalt, one that realises the full possibilities of the medium for releasing his sensate impulse. Without a feel for the expressive flow and tension of words, the meanings of words make the child feel as foolish and clumsy as he might do trying to make a 'photographic' likeness to a person when he has no feel for the use of light and line.

For music teachers the method may seem particularly strange as a result of the strongly instrumental bias of music training. Nevertheless, creative music relies on the same creative process as all the other arts, and exactly the same use can be made of that process within the music lesson. For example, the teacher might get pupils working in pairs to enact a quarrel making use of only one sound which may be long or short and repeated in different rhythmic sequences at different pitches. The contrasts, and polarities of the argument can be explored as a complete episode that has a beginning, a development, and a conclusion. Once the pupil has grasped the sensate problem in the experience of the changes in pitch and rhythm, etc., that accompany the development of the argument he can be encouraged to make a holding form for an expressive act that makes use of the same gestalt. For instance the teacher may require the pupils to express the sensate problem through the medium of a 'storm at sea' or of the 'birth trauma'. Following this the pupil may work with successive approximations, elaborating the same basic gestalt through successive approximations to a resolution. The earliest approximations might make use of natural sound, and the later approximations of instrumental sound. Rhythm pitch, and harmony would also be worked up in the approximations until relatively fine control of the medium was obtained. Again, the only constraints are that each approximation should represent a finer level of medium control than the one that preceded it, and that each approximation should embody the gestalt of the sensate problem.

The three phases of the creative process which I have termed the 'setting of the sensate problem', the 'making of a holding form,' and the 'movement through successive approximations to a resolution', offer a possibility for ending the externality of the teacher's praxis to the pupil's expressive act. Because the teacher enters the creative process from the outset with the sensate problem, his praxis can become involved within the pupil's expressive act. The sensate problem embodies the gestalt which appears in each of the ensuing expressive acts of the pupil until the resolution form is reached. In this way arts teachers can come to work closely with the young in the development of the crowning achievement of mental life, the intelligence of feeling.

The most perfect freedom imaginable is the utter stillness of unimpeded motion. We feel life, however, in resistance and impediment. Only in the inner act of reciprocation that lies at the heart of the creative moment is something known which is akin to the most perfect freedom imaginable. How strange and alarming is talk of freedom in the mouths of those who have never known it! Listen quietly to it, and you will hear a snarl to drain your life's blood. Talk of freedom stalks our urban industrial jungles. It permeates our schools and universities, and a dull anxiety creeps over many of those who work in them. Talk of freedom is heady stuff. It is safest in the mouths of those who have known it. To say that man needs freedom is to say that he needs the creative moment and the act of reciprocation within it. When the educational encounter comes to be seen as a vast sequence of creative moments then we will produce a generation that has known freedom and can use it, a generation that knows what it really means to insist upon oneself.

Select Bibliography

1   **Arts education**

English

ABBS, PETER, *English for Diversity*, Heinemann Educational Books, 1969.
BARNES, DOUGLAS, BRITTON, JAMES, ROSEN, HAROLD, and the L.A.T.E.,
    Language, the Learner and the School, Penguin, 1969.
BECKETT, JACK, *The Keen Edge*, Blackie, 1965.
CLEGG, A. B., *The Excitement of Writing*, Chatto & Windus, 1964.
CREBER, J. W. P., *Sense and Sensitivity*, University of London Press, 1965.
CUTFORTH, J. A. and BATTERSBY, S. H., *Children and Books*, Blackwell, 1962.
FISHER, MARGERY, *Intent upon Reading*, Brockhampton, 1964.
FOWLER, F. D., *Language and Emotion*, Longman, 1966.
HOLBROOK, DAVID, *The Exploring World*, Cambridge University Press,
    1967.
HOLBROOK, DAVID, *The Secret Places*, Methuen, 1964.
HOLBROOK, DAVID, *English for the Rejected*, Cambridge University Press,
    1964.
HOLBROOK, DAVID, *English for Maturity*, Cambridge University Press,
    1961.
HOURD, M. L., *Some Emotional Aspects of Learning*, Heinemann Educa-
    tional Books, 1951.
JACKSON, BRIAN, *English versus Examinations*, Chatto & Windus, 1965.

Select Bibliography

MARLAND, MICHAEL, *Towards the New Fifth*, Longman, 1969.

MATTAM, DONALD, *The Vital Approach*, Macmillan, 1963.

OWENS, GRAHAM, and MARLAND, MICHAEL (eds)., *The Practice of English Teaching*, Blackie, 1970.

STEINER, GEORGE, *Language and Silence*, Penguin, 1969.

STEVENS, FRANCES, *English and Examinations*, Hutchinson Educational, 1970.

STEVENS, ROY, *An Approach to Literature*, Longman, 1966.

SUMMERFIELD, GEOFFREY, and TUNNICLIFFE, STEVEN (eds.), *English in Practice*, Cambridge University Press, 1971.

THOMPSON, DENYS, and JACKSON, BRIAN, *English in Education*, Chatto & Windus, 1962.

WALSH, J. H., *Teaching English*, Heinemann Educational Books, 1965.

WHITEHEAD, FRANK, *The Disappearing Dais*, Chatto & Windus, 1966.

WILKINSON, ANDREW, *The Foundations of Language*, Oxford University Press, 1971.

Art

BARKAN, MANUEL, *Curriculum in Art Education*—Seminar in Art Education for Research and Curriculum Development, Pennsylvania State University, Sept., 1965.

BARKAN, MANUEL, 'Transition in Art Education—Changing Conceptions of Curriculum Content and Teaching', *Art Education*, Vol. XV, pp. 12–18, Oct. 1962.

BARKAN, MANUEL, CHAPMAN, L. H., and KERN, E. J., *Guidelines*, CEMREL, 1970.

CHURCHILL, A. R., *Art for Preadolescents*, McGraw-Hill, 1971.

DEPARTMENT OF EDUCATION AND SCIENCE, *Education Survey II—Art in Schools*, H.M.S.O., 1971.

EISNER, E. W., *Readings in Art Education*, Blaisdell Publishing Co., 1966.

EISNER, E. W., 'Toward a New Era in Art Education', *Studies in Art Education*, Vol. 6, No. 2, Spring 1965.

EISNER, E. W., 'Art Education' in *Encyclopaedia of Educational Research*, Collier-Macmillan, 1969.

FIELD, DICK, *Change in Art Education*, Routledge & Kegan Paul, 1970.

HANNEMA, SJOERD, *Fads, Fakes and Fantasies*, Macdonald, 1970.

HOGG, JAMES, *Psychology and the Visual Arts*, Penguin, 1969.

KELLOGG, RHODA, *Analysing Children's Art*, National Press Books, 1969.

KLEE, PAUL, *The Thinking Eye* (Notebooks, Vol. 1), Lund, Humphries & Co. Ltd., 1961.

LANIER, VINCENT, *Teaching Secondary Art*, International Textbook Co., 1964.

MCFEE, J. K., *Preparation for Art,* Wadsworth Publishing Co., Inc., 1961.

MANZELLA, DAVID, *Educationists and the Evisceration of the Visual Arts,* International Textbook Co., 1963.

MATTIL, E. L. (ed.), *A Seminar in Art Education for Research and Curriculum Development,* U.S. Dept. of Health, Education and Welfare, Office of Education, Co-operative Research Project No. V-002, Pennsylvania State University, 1966.

MOHOLY-NAGY, LASZLO, *The New Vision,* Wittenborn, 1947.

MOHOLY-NAGY, LASZLO, *Painting, Photography, Film,* Lund, Humphries, 1969.

PALMER, FREDERICK, *Art and the Young Adolescent,* Pergamon, 1970.

PORTCHMOUTH, J., *Secondary School Art,* Studio Vista, 1971.

READ, HERBERT, *Education through Art,* Faber & Faber, 1961.

RICHARDSON, MARION, *Art and the Child,* University of London Press, 1948.

ROWLAND, K., *Looking and Seeing*: Books 1-4 (with Teachers' Notes), Ginn, 1964.

SAUSMAREZ, Maurice de, *Basic Design,* Studio Vista, 1964.

SCOTTISH EDUCATION DEPARTMENT, *Art in Secondary Schools,* Edinburgh: H.M.S.O., 1971.

SMITH, R. A., *Aesthetics and Criticism in Art Education,* Rand, McNally 1966.

THOMPSON, SIR D'ARCY, *On Growth and Form,* Cambridge University Press, 1966.

TSUGAWA, ALBERT, 'The Nature of the Aesthetic and Human Values', *Art Education,* Vol. 21, pp. 9-15, Nov., 1968.

WEITZ, M., 'The Nature of Art' in *Readings in Art Education,* edited by E. W. Eisner and D. W. Ecker, Waltham, 1966.

Drama

ARTS COUNCIL OF GREAT BRITAIN, *The Provision of Theatre for Young People,* Arts Council, 1966.

CHILVER, PETER, *Improvised Drama,* Batsford, 1967.

DEPARTMENT OF EDUCATION AND SCIENCE, *Drama* in 'Education Survey 2', H.M.S.O., 1969.

DEPARTMENT OF EDUCATION AND SCIENCE, *Drama in Education,* Reports on Education, No. 50, Nov. 1968.

DODD, NIGEL, and HICKSON, WINIFRED, *Drama and Theatre in Education,* Heinemann Educational Books, 1971.

HEATHCOTE, DOROTHY, 'How does Drama serve Thinking, Talking and Writing?', *Elementary English,* 47, pp.1077-81, Dec. 1970.

HODGSON, JOHN, and RICHARDS, ERNEST, *Improvisation: Discovery and Creativity in Drama,* Methuen, 1966.

PEMBERTON-BILLING, R. N., and CLEGG, J. D., *Teaching Drama,* University of London Press, 1965.

SLADE, PETER, *An Introduction to Child Drama,* University of London Press, 1967.

SLADE, PETER, *Experience of Spontaneity,* Longman, 1968.

SLADE, PETER, *Children's Theatre and Theatre for Young People,* Educational Drama Association, 1968.

SLADE, PETER, *et al.,* 'The Teaching of Drama', *Higher Educational Journal,* 17, pp. 10–26, Summer 1970.

SLADE, PETER, 'Drama and the Middle School: Report as from the Educational Drama Association for the Middle Years of Schooling Research Project', University of Lancaster Educational Drama Assoc., 1971.

WAY, BRIAN, *Development through Drama,* Longman, 1967.

Music

ALVIN, JULIETTE, *Music Therapy,* John Baker, 1966.

BROUDY, HARRY, 'A Realistic Philosophy of Music Education—Basic Concepts in Music Education', *National Society for the Study of Education,* Vol. LVII, Part 1, 1958.

DENNIS, BRIAN, *Experimental Music in Schools,* Oxford University Press, 1970.

DEPARTMENT OF EDUCATION AND SCIENCE, *Music and the Young,* D.E.S. Reports on Education, No. 39, Sept. 1967.

DEPARTMENT OF EDUCATION AND SCIENCE, *Music in Schools,* Report, 2nd edition, H.M.S.O., 1969.

DEPARTMENT OF EDUCATION AND SCIENCE, *Creative Music in Schools,* D.E.S. Reports on Education No. 63, April 1970.

DOBBS, J. P. B., *The Slow Learner and Music—A Handbook for Teachers,* Oxford University Press, 1966.

MELLERS, WILFRID, *Music and Society,* Dennis Dobson, 1946.

MELLERS, WILFRID, *Music in a New Found Land,* Barrie & Rockliff, 1964.

MELLERS, WILFRID, *Caliban Reborn—Renewal in 20th Century Music,* Gollancz, 1968.

NORDOFF, PAUL, and ROBBINS, CLIVE, *Therapy in Music for Handicapped Children,* Gollancz, 1971.

PAYNTER, JOHN, and ASTON, PETER, *Sound and Silence—Classroom Projects in Creative Music,* Cambridge University Press, 1970.

REIMER, BENNETT, 'A New Curriculum for Secondary General Music', *Bulletin of the Council for Research in Music Education,* No. 4, pp. 11–20, Winter 1965.

SCHNEIDER, E., 'Music Education' in *Encyclopaedia of Educational Research,* Collier-Macmillan, 1969.

SCHOOLS COUNCIL, *Music and the Young School Leaver,* Evans/Methuen Educational, 1971.
SWANWICK, KEITH, *Popular Music and the Teacher,* Pergamon, 1968.

Dance

LABAN, RUDOLF, *The Mastery of Movement,* N.Y. D.B.S. Publications, 1960.
LABAN, RUDOLF, *Modern Educational Dance,* Macdonald & Evans, 1964.
NORTH, MARION, *Introduction to Movement Study and Teaching,* Macdonald & Evans, 1971.
RUSSELL, JOAN, *Modern Dance in Education,* Praeger, 1958.

Film

ARNHEIM, RUDOLF, *Film as Art,* Faber & Faber, 1958.
BRITISH FILM INSTITUTE, *The Cinema: A Short Booklist,* B.F.I. Education Dept.
BRITISH FILM INSTITUTE, *Study of Film—A Study of Approaches,* B.F.I., 1967–68.
LOWNDES, DOUGLAS, *Film Making in Schools,* Batsford, 1968.
RUSSELL TAYLOR, J., *Cinema Eye: Cinema Ear,* Methuen, 1964.

2 Curriculum development

BLOOM, B. S. (ed.), *et al, Taxonomy of Educational Objectives: Handbook 1, Cognitive Domain,* Longman, 1956.
BLOOM, B. S., *et al, Taxonomy of Educational Objectives: Handbook 2, Affective Domain,* Longman, 1964.
HIRST, P. H., and PETERS, R. S., *The Logic of Education,* Routledge & Kegan Paul, 1970.
HOOPER, RICHARD (ed), *The Curriculum: Context, Design and Development Readings,* edited for the Course Team at the Open University, Oliver & Boyd, 1971.
MUSGROVE, F., 'Curriculum Objectives', *Journal of Curriculum Studies,* Vol. 1, No. 1, Nov. 1968.
O.E.C.D., *Modernising our Schools: Curriculum Improvement and Educational Development,* Paris, Dec. 1966.
PHENIX, PHILIP H., *Realms of Meaning: A Philosophy of the Curriculum for General Education,* McGraw-Hill, 1964.
PIDGEON, D., and WISEMAN, S., *Curriculum Evaluation,* National Foundation for Educational Research, 1970.
RICHMOND, K. W., *The School Curriculum,* Methuen, 1971.
ROBINSON, S., 'A Conceptual Structure of Curriculum Development', *Comparative Education,* Vol. 5, No. 3, Dec. 1969—a paper read at the fourth biennial meeting of the Comparative Education Society

in Europe, whose general theme was 'Curriculum Development in Europe at the Second Level of Education'.

SCRIVEN, M., 'The Methodology of Evaluation' in *Perspectives of Curriculum Evaluation* edited by R. W. Tyler, R. M. Gagné and M. Scriven, AERA Monographs on Curriculum Evaluation, No. 1, Rand McNally, 1967.

TABA, H., *Curriculum Development: Theory and Practice,* Harcourt Brace, 1962.

3 Related general reading

ALBRECHT, M. C., BARNETT, J. H., and GRIFF, M. (eds.), *The Sociology of Art and Literature,* Duckworth, 1970.

ALVAREZ, A., *The Savage God,* Weidenfeld & Nicolson, 1971.

ANDERSON, JOHN M., *The Realm of Art,* Pennsylvania State University Press, 1967.

ARNHEIM, RUDOLF, *Art and Visual Perception,* Faber, 1956.

ARNHEIM, RUDOLF, *Toward a Psychology of Art,* University of California Press, 1966.

ARNHEIM, RUDOLF, *Visual Thinking,* Faber, 1970.

ARTS COUNCIL OF GREAT BRITAIN, *The Arts and the Community,* Arts Council, 1970.

BERNSTEIN, BASIL, 'On the Classification and Framing of Educational Knowledge', in *Knowledge and Control,* edited by M. Young, Collier-Macmillan, 1971.

BERNSTEIN, BASIL, 'Open Schools, Open Society?', *New Society,* 14 Sept. 1967.

BOLAM, D. W., and HENDERSON, J. L., *Art and Belief,* Hamish Hamilton, 1968.

BRUNER, JEROME S., *On Knowing—Essays for the Left Hand,* Harvard University Press, 1962.

BRUNER, JEROME S., *The Process of Education,* Harvard University Press, 1966.

BRUNER, JEROME S., *Toward a Theory of Instruction,* Harvard University Press, 1966.

COOMBS, P. H., *The World Educational Crisis: A Systems Analysis,* Oxford University Press, 1968.

DEPARTMENT OF EDUCATION AND SCIENCE, *Statistics of Education: Special Series—Survey of the Curriculum and Deployment of Teachers (Secondary Schools),* 1965–66, Part 1, H.M.S.O., 1968.

DEWEY, JOHN, *Art as Experience,* Minton, Balch & Co., 1934.

DUNCAN, NEIL S., *The Arts in the South,* Southern Arts Association, 1970.

ECKER, D. W., 'The Artistic Process as Qualitative Problem Solving', *Journal of Aesthetics and Art Criticism,* **XXI**, iii, Spring 1963.

The Intelligence of Feeling

EHRENZWEIG, ANTON, *The Hidden Order of Art,* Weidenfeld & Nicolson, 1967.

ERICKSON, R., 'Youth in Conflict', *Journal of Secondary Education,* **43,** pp. 16–18, Jan. 1968.

ERIKSON, E. H., *Identity, Youth and Crisis,* Faber & Faber, 1971.

ESTIMATES COMMITTEE to the House of Commons, *Grants to the Arts*—8th Report, London, 1960.

FLAVELL, JOHN H., *The Developmental Psychology of Jean Piaget*(Foreword by Jean Piaget), D. Van Nostrand, 1963.

FROMM, ERICH, *The Heart of Man,* Routledge & Kegan Paul, 1965.

GAGNE, ROBERT M., *The Conditions of Learning,* Holt, Rinehart & Winston, 1965.

GALLIE, W. B., 'Art as an Essentially Contested Concept', *Philadelphia Quarterly,* **6,** pp. 97–114, 1956.

GIEDION, S., *Mechanization takes Command,* Oxford University Press, 1948.

GOVERNMENT WHITE PAPER, *A Policy for the Arts: The First Steps,* H.M.S.O., 1965.

GREEN, MICHAEL, and WILDING, MICHAEL, *Cultural Policies in Britain: a Report to UNESCO,* Centre for Contemporary Cultural Studies, 1969. (Unpublished.)

GROPIUS, WALTER, *Apollo in the Democracy: the Cultural Obligation of the Architect,* McGraw-Hill, 1968.

HENRY, JULES, *Culture against Man,* Tavistock, 1966.

HIMMELWEIT, DR. H., OPPENHEIM, A., and VINCE, P., *Television and the Child,* Oxford University Press, 1958.

HUDSON, LIAM, *Contrary Imaginations—a Psychological Study of the English Schoolboy,* Methuen, 1966.

ILLICH, IVAN, *Deschooling Society,* Calder & Boyers, 1971.

ITTEN, JOHANNES, *Design and Form—the Basic Course at the Bauhaus,* Thames & Hudson, 1964.

JACKSON, BRIAN, and MCALHONE, BERYL, *Verdict on the Facts—the Case for Educational Change* Advisory Centre for Education, 1969.

JONES, RICHARD, *Fantasy and Feeling in Education,* University of London Press, 1968.

KAHLER, E., 'What is Art?', in *Problems in Aesthetics,* edited by M. Weitz, Macmillan, N.Y., 1959.

KANDINSKY, WASSILY, *Concerning the Spiritual in Art,* Wittenborn, 1947.

KEPES, GYORGY, *Language of Vision,* Paul Theobold, 1944.

KEPES, GYORGY, *The New Landscape in Art and Science,* Paul Theobald & Co., 1956.

KEPES, GYORGY, *Structure in Art and Science,* Studio Vista, 1965.

KEPES, GYORGY, *Education of Vision,* Studio Vista, 1965.

KEPES, GYORGY, *Sign, Image and Symbol,* Studio Vista, 1966.

KEPES, GYORGY, *The Man-Made Object,* Studio Vista, 1966.

KETTLE, ARNOLD, *The Arist and Society*—Humanities Course, Unit 4, The Open Universities Press, 1970.

LAING, R. D., and PHILLIPSON, H., *Interpersonal Perception,* Tavistock Publications, 1966.

LAING, R. D., *The Politics of Experience and the Bird of Paradise,* Penguin, 1967.

LAING, R. D., *Self and Others,* 2nd edition, Tavistock Publications, 1969.

LAMBERT, S., 'Music and Art in the Public Schools', *Art Education,* **XVI**, Dec. 1963.

LANGER, SUZANNE K., 'The Cultural Importance of the Arts', in *Aesthetic Form and Education* edited by M. Andrews, Syracuse University Press, 1958.

LANGER, SUZANNE K., *Feeling and Form,* Routledge & Kegal Paul, 1953.

LANGER, SUZANNE K., *Philosophy in a New Key,* Harvard University Press, 1967.

LAUWERYS, JOSEPH (ed.), *The World Year Book of Education* 1969: *Examinations,* Evans, 1969.

LYTTON, HUGH, *Creativity and Education,* Routledge & Kegan Paul, 1971.

MCLUHAN, MARSHALL, and PARKER, HARLEY, *Through the Vanishing Point: Space in Poetry and Painting,* Harper & Row, 1969.

MARLAND, MICHAEL, *Towards the New Fifth,* Longman, 1969.

MASLOW, ABRAHAM H., *Motivation and Personality,* Harper & Row, 2nd edition, 1970.

MASLOW, ABRAHAM H., *Toward a Psychology of Being,* Van Nostrand Reinhold, 1968.

MOUSTAKAS, CLARK E., *The Self,* Harper & Row, 1956.

MUSGROVE, F., *Patterns of Power and Authority in English Education,* Methuen, 1971.

NEWSOM REPORT, *Half our Future,* H.M.S.O., 1963.

OSBORNE, HAROLD, *The Oxford Companion to Art,* Oxford University Press, 1970.

OSBORNE, HAROLD, *The Art of Appreciation,* Oxford University Press, 1970.

P.E.P. REPORT, *Public Patronage to the Arts,* London, 1965.

READ, HERBERT, *The Meaning of Art,* Pitman, 1951.

READ, HERBERT, *The Grassroots of Art,* Faber, 1955.

READ, HERBERT, *The Forms of Things Unknown,* Faber, 1960.

READ, HERBERT, *The Redemption of the Robot: My Encounter with Education through Art,* Trident Press, 1966.

REID, LOUIS ARNAUD, *Meaning in the Arts,* George Allen & Unwin, 1969.

RICHMOND, KENNETH, *Culture and General Education,* Methuen University Paperbacks, 1964.

SCHACHTEL, ERNEST G., *Metamorphosis,* Routledge & Kegan Paul, 1963.

SCHOOLS COUNCIL, *Enquiry 1: The Young School Leavers,* H.M.S.O., 1968.

SCHOOLS COUNCIL, Examination Bulletin No. 20, *CSE: A Group Study Approach to Research and Development,* Evans/Methuen Educational, 1970.

SCHOUVALOFF, ALEXANDER (ed.), *Place for the Arts,* North West Arts Association, Seel House Press, 1970.

SMITH, R. A. (ed.), *Aesthetic Concepts and Education,* University of Illinois Press, 1970.

SPARSHOTT, F. E., *The Structure of Aesthetics,* Routledge & Kegan Paul, 1963.

TAYLOR, L. C., *Resources for Learning,* Penguin, 1971.

TAYLOR, WILLIAM, *Half a Million Teachers,* University of Bristol, 1968.

TUCKER, NICHOLAS, *Understanding the Mass Media,* Cambridge University Press, 1966.

UNESCO, *The Arts and Man: a World View of the Role and Functions of the Arts in Society,* H.M.S.O., 1969.

WEITZ, M., *Problems in Aesthetics,* Macmillan, N.Y., 1959.

WHANNEL, P., and HALL, STUART, *The Popular Arts,* Hutchinson, 1964.

WOLLHEIM, RICHARD, *Art and its Objects,* Penguin, 1970.